COMPLETE BULL

My journey to connect mind, body and soul

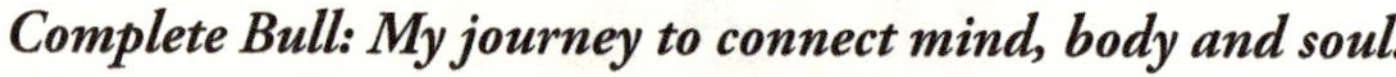

www.DigitalAlphabet.com

COMPLETE BULL

My journey to connect mind, body and soul

Brian J. Mueller

DIGITAL ALPHABET BOOKS

CONTENTS

Introduction

Thank you for picking up this copy of *Complete Bull: My journey to connect mind, body and soul.* I hope you appreciate the title in the tongue-in-cheek sense it is intended. This book is a compilation of my earlier works, *Bull Head* (2002), *Bull Heart* (2015) and *More Bull* (2016). I wanted to publish them in a single volume because I believe they tell the story of my maturation from the heady and romantic dreamer I was in my youth, through the trying disappointments as I entered middle age, and now onward into a personal humility and easier appreciation of my experiences.

• • •

Bull Head (mind) is a compilation of both poetry and prose from the ten years after I graduated high school. While growing up I never considered writing poetry, even though I harbored romantic dreams of becoming the next Hemingway. Nonetheless, I suppose I started writing poetry and short prose because it is a skill respected by my family members, and because I was lucky to receive a liberal arts education which valued many types of artistic expression.

At this time in my life it is easy for me to see the naiveté and romance within my earliest writings. I was clearly trying to make sense of this world and of my place in it. I could feel the strength of my physicality, which I believe is displayed in my prose and poetry as an assuredness and certain optimism about life. So much in life was new, most of all the possibilities of love and the adult world now open to me for exploration. My verse rhymed because that was my understanding of the order of things, and because I was enchanted by my own clever turns of phrase.

My earliest poems stand testament to my desire to enjoy life. Yet I had little idea of what was to come. When I published *Bull Head,* I was certain the ink would not stop flowing and that new collections of poetry and fantastic novels would be quickly forthcoming. But of course, that's rarely how things play out. Almost immediately after publication I realized I had left one epoch of my life behind and a new one was about to emerge.

• • •

I'm certainly not alone in struggling through the trauma in my experience of 9/11. Even today I'm still struggling to grasp the tragedy of this event both personally and for our country as a whole. I'll never board an airplane with the same sense of easiness I once did. And I'll never again see myself at the center of anything, but rather as a tiny part of something much larger. Whatever innocence of being I had clung to, it disappeared in the years after 2001. Though I continued scribbling in notebooks, for many years I lost my voice.

It turns out, in the decade after the publication *Bull Head* I had a lot of growing up to do. Like many of my high school friends, I moved closer to home where I ventured into radio and neighborhood activism. I had a lot of things I wanted to say, but the world didn't seem to need what I had to share. So I stumbled along and did what many people do and got married. For a few years this became the very reason for my existence, and then suddenly it too was no more. Devastated, I collapsed into total darkness.

Sometimes the desire to continue living takes the shape of a single breath, and then another. Marriage taught me a great many things, but I didn't appreciate the lesson until I was divorced. So began the journey that culminated in *Bull Heart* (soul), a collection of poems that came out of the grief and darkness of my struggle to be reborn.

It took great humility and the discovery that everywhere there is invisible help, for me to connect my head and my heart. In the years after my divorce I turned to everyone and everything for answers. I found great witnesses to the mysterious beauty of life and began to assuage my anger by writing about my feelings. I also spent a great deal of time closer to nature in the forests and mountains, which not only delighted my senses, but gave me a great deal of perspective about my own insignificance and my own individual beauty. Succinctly, *Bull Head* is a poetic journey through the process of discovering my soul.

• • •

At my high school, there was a placard near the main entrance that read, "Man's mind, once stretched by a new idea, never regains its original dimensions."[1] I now know this was just a seed for the students to gather, and was offered in the hope it would eventually bear the fruit of great realization. Recalling these words today helps me to understand the transformation of body and soul which was necessary for me to accept my mortality and to see my gifts anew.

More Bull (body) is a collection of everyday poems dedicated to the men and women on their own epic journey through life. It contains poems written as part of my daily practice of meditation. In these verses I embrace others like never before, and find a great deal of inspiration in their own stories and poetry.

My poems have always been very intimate and personal, and yet I hope they now speak more broadly to the common experiences we all share. Poetry has become my language for communicating with God and for bringing me closer to those things I cannot comprehend. Not every poem I write is profound and mystical. Some poke fun and remind me not to take life too seriously. At the very least, I hope my poems will remind others of the simple beauty and mystery of everyday life.

• • •

So it is with a bit of trepidation I publish *Complete Bull.* I see this as the end of my first half of life journey to connect mind, body and soul (heart). Though I have crossed over into a much larger universe, I realize that my journey is ongoing. Just as there will be no end to the challenges I must face, so too there will be no end to the beauty and mystery of my life. I pray only for the desire and strength to continue towards new horizons…

Brian (2017)

P.S. I offer a daily poem to readers in their email inbox. You can learn more and subscribe for free at http://poem.digitalalphabet.com.

---

1 Quote attributed to Oliver Wendell Holmes, Jr.

To this life and to the essential mystery!

"Since love grows within you, so beauty grows.
For love is the beauty of the soul."

—Augustine of Hippo

for Melissa

BULL HEAD

The Selected Writings of Brian J. Mueller 1991-2001

Contents

Right there I felt it.
Now it is almost gone.
My mind let go of my body,
So my body wrote a song.

Bull Head Introduction

Several years ago, at the first publication of this collection of my writings in 2002, I wrote the following introduction:

> *The time has come for me to share a selection of the writings from the years immediately following my high school education. In these pages you will find some prose, and even more poetry. I would caution at times my writing is simplistic and may even lack the polish of more experienced writers. Yet I believe as you read further you will notice an evolution in style and clarity, which in the future I shall endeavor to develop.*
>
> *Despite the very personal nature of these works, my intention has always been to publish them. As I look back over this volume of writings, I am sometimes a little embarrassed and surprised by my own naiveté. But if there were no merit to the ideas and beliefs I explore here I would not have undertaken such an effort to print them.*
>
> *As you embark upon these pages it is important for me to note that while my motivation to write is internal, further inspiration comes from my family, friends, mentors, and more. I sincerely expect you'll enjoy the material and any feedback you have is welcome.*

Since then my understanding of this body of work has changed dramatically. For starters, I no longer feel a sense of shyness or embarrassment about my work. As I originally prepared this text for publication, I wondered why anyone might want to read poems and prose about my experiences and feelings. I realized a great deal of the emotions I described are common to us all, but I did not understand the sense of community, of genuine human connection and understanding that can be gained through the exchange of words. Perhaps I was jaded by all the bluster coming at us from the airwaves and the Internet.

Today I am very proud of this volume. My goal was to make my writings available and accessible for friends and family. Little did I know that its publication would also symbolically mark the closing of one chapter of my life and the beginning of a new one. Since the arrival of *Bull Head* I have done very little writing, but I have not stopped feeling, experiencing, and challenging myself with very important questions.

It is true that everyone has a voice. This voice changes literally and metaphorically with the passage of time. Many express their voices through creativity and vocation. Others find their voice in more subtle ways, but universally we all need to be heard and understood. For it seems the silencing of this voice becomes frustration and quite possibly something worse. The writings in this volume are my voice for a particular period of my life. It gives me great pleasure to share them with you.

Brian (2007)

PROSE

Edge of Sanity

I am sitting here on the edge of your sanity. Dare cross and your eternity will be altogether different. I do not promise me, nor do I expect you. Hope runs rampant in my world. Here you can be true to yourself, and open in your love. There are risks, and there are hazards. The price is no more than death, and the reward is no less than everlasting love. Step back and you risk little. I invite you to step up.

(*One more thing: Death is a peaceful love of blue-brown-eyed people with hysterical laughs and soft, gentle, meaningful features.*)

Our First Conversation

If I had to describe her I'd say she is like the sun. She has a burning rough edge and stunning brilliance. Her passion is white hot. Her light is focused. Still, there are spots, little openings, visible vulnerabilities. These "wounds" pour forth her life. She is the Sun because she brings out the best in me, the Earth. I thrive on her light, and my thoughts spin about her. I long for her touch, but I fear the burn. However, I smile because I know she longs to have her cares soothed in my cool waters.

She resists, I insist. If we could go it alone we would not need our hands. Idle fire spills from within her. Change comes so slowly, and yet time measures it fast. She feels spirits; she wants them to be free. She knows I am the one she longs to see…

Brian & Honor

Tonight Fate smiles upon Honor and Brian. We, your family and friends, applaud the commitment you have made to each other and celebrate your willingness to follow a beckoning love. Yet let us always remember that love does not possess, nor would it be possessed. Love is a double-edged sword that demands you remain true to one another or suffer greatly.

Here's to you, Brian and Honor. May your love not become a rusty chain that binds you together, but a river flowing freely from sea to sea, soul to soul…

Cheers!

New Aristocracy

We drank beer in the hot sun of a Reds game as the vendors hustled back and forth with their coolers and the umpires barked calls from the field which rolled out beneath us, our gaze falling symmetrically from the red seats to the yellow, green, and finally the blue where the wealthier patrons of the game sat idly chatting about their finances and sipping their margaritas with straws that looked like the peppermint sticks we would lick in front of a roaring Christmas fire. Among them was Fesum Ogbazion.

Furious Passion

She swims through the synapses of my mind, a very crowded place. I think about everything, and only her. She is not alone, but comes with much. And her absence—in that is much.

If I were to give her a name it would be "Passion," for I have none. I keep mine bottled up, never daring to let the light of day hit it. I do not need to; I live vicariously through all of her large nuances and extremes.

I love her, because if I do not I will hate everything. Hate makes me destroy; I do not wish to destroy anything.

Everything and everyone is inside of me. And I am inside of them. That is her secret; this is her saving grace.

Southern California Thoughts

Everyone is trying to live up to this image. Only thing is no one is quite sure how the rest of the world perceives Californians, and so this image is somewhat unique and distorted among the people.

A Gray Hair

Like lightning across my brow, the gray struck. As I stood, young and strong against the wind, it sailed free. I did not notice it; a friend did. She quickly snatched my silver like a thief in a crowd. A moment of shock, a moment to blush, and a moment to laugh—gone. Now only the brown tresses remain echoing the fire within. Lightning will certainly strike again. Will I even let myself notice it?

Self Portrait (1)

He is really a rather simple man. Do not be fooled by the reserved exterior or deceptive smile. He lacks the ability to ignore his senses, though his rational powers are great. Never have I met anyone with a greater ability to translate the most complex of ideas or devices into simple terms for all to understand. He is a philosopher who can communicate clearly, a technician with feeling.

Lemon-Lime

They were out of lemons, and so she gave me limes. And it turns out that trying limes in my iced tea was one of the best improbabilities to come along in life. Having come to grips with this new taste, I am free to ponder the snaring of a woman's affections.

Cordiform LA Button

I stepped off the sand and onto the strand. I looked down at my shadow and saw Caesar's commanding presence: the legacy of Rome alive and well standing fierce under the L.A. Sun.

That is what I remember most vividly. Except I can also remember the evening spent in San Juan Capistrano where the band rocked a small bar singing about lions and silver spaceships, not even whispering about the bag of groceries taken off the shelf too early. But I did not mind, at least at first. I was spending my time waiting, watching, and wondering. Time is not time when spent with good friends. We drank (me enjoying the best fountain cola I had ever tasted). I bellowed that I could not fight the feeling. My friends laughed, but they knew I was holding back. About that time a drunken miser stumbled on top of me, and it was all I could do to suppress the seething, yellow rage. Afterwards I sat in compliance, even during the conga.

My thoughts stripped away reality and I was in a world where women wore no clothes and I could breathe deep in self-fulfillment. And in that dream world lived the girl I had written on the plane (over the plains); strange, aloof, never fitting, like the wrong size screwdriver. And lest I sell her short, I must reveal that she, my first heart-stopper, possessed a beauty rivaled only by her intelligence. But I dribble...

Then I visited the only girl that dragged me to the edge of love. (Stopped cold I was, but I am still too young and inexperienced to know why.) Of course everything inside of me was present there, but I only noticed the sacrifices I made now and would in the future as I pondered my crossroads, especially that Western Path.

Heavy Metal

Allow me to describe how much I miss California and the warm desire…

Heavy metal speaks volumes to the black masses. (You should see how brilliant the players really are! A combination of Gershwin, Beethoven, Copeland with Vulcan's fiery hammer, they rival the most serious musicologist.)

You can't fool me with that sharp-ass smile and rolling left eye. The smell is a tearing yellow, wet leather, and I don't remember your breath but I can see and hear you inhale, holding tight longer and longer until your lungs collapse and the sound in your throat grows louder and more excited. And I am reminded of your success in scaring me with that unanticipated response. For at that moment I realized why it is a man would build a castle for his bride, and why he would put it on the greenest rolling hills with ancient stones and the skillful mist everywhere clinging to the life that is her. Ah, but you paralyze my truest sense that lives on the edge of darkness and rages at the slightest injustice. Please don't stop me before I write a song for those demons of leather. Simple lyrics are all they need, and for you who want the straight and forward song without conjunctions, well, I will kiss you. No more plain and simple can I be. Hopefully when I bite your lip so gently, the smell of your breath like the musk in a damp autumn forest will extinguish this burning desire to flee westward and wayward. For in that heavy metal song of Harvard Yard love is the elixir that will keep Nebraska poets and saguaro prophets from ranging toward the setting sun and the California Seductress.

Waiting

Not even a simple "Fuck you!" But maybe you don't know yet. The waiting is killing me. All this bullshit about John Glenn, and I'm dying 'cause I might see you on the news. And the pain of not being at your side—you excited by the launch, the legacy, and the romance. Me, seduced by your mortality—a lust so primal. It is a gray day here. Nothing can fill my life like you, so I wander aimlessly through my apartment finding small projects. Finally I've had enough, and before I rue the day I was born, I set sail for the library. I crave the peopled solace and the solitude of my study. Why do I feel so anxious? I want to swallow it whole—the world, her, everything! Leonard Bernstein could not simply be a gay man. I cannot only be a writer, technician, teacher, handyman, lover… Take one away and I am gone. I am the gift life gives itself, the appreciation of so much diversity, the adroit realization of human frailty, and the conscious desire to become better. But oh the burden this places on my carbon shoulders. I want to be the man on television with the bourbon in one hand and the cigarette in the other, with the "fuck 'em all" cowboy mentality that sells millions of books, tickets, videos, whatever. And so this has become my everyday and my every night. I can't remember a time when I didn't try to devour the entire universe. Will I find salvation in her reply? Oh most divine creature please let me die.

I need a little hollow place inside my sanity where I can splash.

He had always been there she thought.

He had always been there she thought. I know that I've seen him lurking in the distance. I can hear his voice calling out to friends. Why haven't I noticed him?

Suddenly she was standing next to him. Her heart skipped a beat. People must be magnetic.

He felt her presence immediately. He could smell her, taste her. It was a strange and primal feeling. The hair on his neck stood on end.

A simpler time, a quieter place, and the animal passions would have consumed them. Instead an uneasy awkwardness settled between them and an urgency developed. Speak now or forever hold your peace.

He swallowed hard. His dry tongue stuck to his teeth. Nevertheless he managed to utter, "Hey!" His hand gestured slowly, rising up from his waist. Eye contact had been made.

Dawn

The girl on the train said, "Why do you look at me so sexually? I don't demean you in the same way."

"And why not?" I replied. "Are we not sexual beings? Besides, you hardly know me, and I hardly know you. How many ways can you look at a person that you don't know?"

"I know you," she said.

"No, you don't. You think because you've spoken to my friend and travel partner about our trip that you know me. Is it conceit, or mere assumption?

"Before you get angry, ask yourself if I am really this pretentious, or if it's an act. Perhaps you feel you know me because you know my friend. You think I am either exactly like my friend, or the exact opposite. I would suggest the real me lies somewhere in between.

"So take a look. Is what you see sexually appealing? If so, get to know me better."

"What about you?" she said.

"Are you asking what I think of you, or are you interested in me?"

"Both."

"How about a drink? I'd like to get to know you."

"I'm not sure of your intentions," she smiled.

"Why they're the same as yours. You're looking for a passionate, intense, and deep love affair sustained for eternity."

She nodded, and I extended my hand

What to Ask Your Lady

I suppose I would ask my lady what it feels like to be a woman, 'cause I would really want to know how she felt. If my tone was sincere, I don't think she'd offer me a lot of clichés. She might ask me what it is like to be a man, and I would tell her everything from the physical to the spiritual. I could tell her about the brute strength which courses through the entire body, by way of the veins in the throat and locking at the jaw. And then I would tell her about the helplessness a man feels in such a large and trying world. And I'd also mention that I have a hard time separating myself from my perception of things; even going so far as to forget my appearance. At times I have to remember what I look like to other people. I think back to the person I see in the mirror, and yet I still cannot remember if my hair is long or short, or even my eye color. I hope she would tell me things like that. In fact, I could tell her all about her smell and what color her eyes are, and the sounds she makes in my mind.

Realization (1)

It is at moments such as these when I realize what is meant by "being afraid to live your life." My heart is so big, but the boundaries I place on it so narrow. Days like this one I feel as though I will burst. I must let myself be free, but the more I let go the more sensitive I become. My limits create order, but constrain life. Life is chaos, beautiful chaos. Stories have been written about humans full of love and beauty as well as anger and loathing. The force that prevails depends on so much. It seems that fate lies in me. Big days are ahead.

Life, grant me the ability to grow, the courage to lead, the strength to feel, and the faith to believe.

Why do guys love Led Zeppelin?

"Why do guys love Led Zeppelin?" she asked.

Oh my, such an innocent and inspirational interrogative! Where to begin, my Muse? Please allow me to breathe these words in a simplicity befitting the subject matter.

Led Zeppelin is the sad song blues for men of Northern European ancestry. Genuine human sentiment combined with electrified rhythms borrowed from black mystics form the core of the Led Zeppelin sound. Men don't just listen to a Zeppelin tune—they become it.

Unlike the admiration and understanding of a Pollock masterpiece, Led Zeppelin is not an acquired taste. To appreciate Zeppelin is to revere the beauty of a woman and to feel truly alive. Take away taste, touch, sight, sound, and smell (all rolled into feeling) and the music is silenced.

Raw emotion and animal sensuality/sexuality burns in the lyrics. The echoing guitar and pounding drums drive the listener to frenzy.

How Many More Times*
Oh, Rosie, oh, girl!
Oh, Rosie, oh, girl!
Steal away now, steal away
Steal away baby, steal away
Little Robert Anthony wants to come and play.
Why don't you come to me baby?
Steal away, all right, all right…

Well they call me the hunter, that's my name
They call me the hunter, that's how I got my fame
Ain't no need to hide,
Ain't no need to run
'Cause I've got you in the sights of my……….gun!

Led Zeppelin sings to the average man, slave of this Earth, full of barroom passion.

Over the Hills and Far Away*
Many dreams come true and some have silver linings
I live for my dream and a pocketful of gold.

Led Zeppelin is a new day.

Stairway to Heaven*
If there's a bustle in your hedgerow, don't be alarmed now,
It's just a spring clean for the May queen.
Yes, there are two paths you can go by
But in the long run
There's still time to change the road you're on.

And then there is the poetry.

Kashmir*
Oh let the sun beat down upon my face, stars to fill my dream
I am a traveler of both time and space, to be where I have been
To sit with elders of the gentle race, this world has seldom seen
They talk of days for which they sit and wait and all will be revealed

Talk and song from tongues of lilting grace, whose sounds caress my ear
But not a word I heard could I relate, the story was quite clear
Oh, oh

Of course Led Zeppelin is wise to the wanton women.

Hey, Hey What Can I Do*
In the bars, with the men who play guitars
Singin', drinkin' and rememberin' the times
My little lover does a midnight shift
She's followed around all the time
I guess there's just one thing a-left for me to do
Gonna pack my bags and move on my way
Cause I got a worried mind
Sharin' what I thought was mine
Gonna leave her where the guitars play

And sometimes Led Zeppelin is bad as hell.

Black Dog*

Hey, hey, mama, said the way you move
Gonna make you sweat, gonna make you groove.
Oh, oh, child, way you shake that thing
Gonna make you burn, gonna make you sting.
Hey, hey, baby, when you walk that way
Watch your honey drip, can't keep away.

Led Zeppelin is the essence of a man and the sentimentality that haunts him. So take some time to appreciate their songs. Much of what constitutes a man is also inside a woman and vice versa.

*Source for *lyrics*: http://www.led-zeppelin.com

Craters of the Moon

How do I feel about her?

...Never has a woman been so adept or quick at getting to the essence of who I am. It is a vulnerable feeling, and so I am in love with her. She grips me and rips me with her dreams. The poet within me shatters like fallen glass. I want to hold her tight at Craters of the Moon.

You should not have called me to apologize.

You should not have called to apologize. It only makes me feel worse. Your thoughts, ideas, and feelings are important to me. You bring me seeds and sow them on fertile ground. They become a wrinkle I cannot smooth for you. And that's tough, like falling out of love.

No Superlatives

The Beginning

- ✓ No Superlatives
- ✓ Driftwood
- ✓ Klimt
- ✓ Running
- ✓ Wisconsin
- ✓ Swing Dancing
- ✓ Radio Head

The Middle

Transcend the logical
Logical but never give up the magical
Tough when you are sensitive to think logically
What is the "value" (under capitalism) in feeling?
[My gift of poems is not so "valuable" to you.]

The pleasure in meeting you is mine.

I thank you kindly for the note.

When I stop to think of Nashville,
only beauty comes to mind.

She told me she doesn't believe in superlatives.
She's the prettiest.
She told me she loves swing dancing.
She turned on Radio Head.
She told me she's from Boston.
She talks as though from Wisconsin.
She talks about running marathons.
She likes the idea of driftwood.

The End

Going places and meeting people is nice.
Running into you was serendipitous.

I am glad you are flattered.

I thank you kindly for the note, and I assure you the pleasure in meeting you and sending it is mine.

Nashville will no longer be a country music myth for me;

instead I'll be thinking of old friends, a newly married couple, and this girl who sounds like she is from Wisconsin, but claims to be from Boston (?)!

Now I must assure you that my intentions could not possibly have been purer.

I wish you all the best.

It will be difficult to find another person who:

- ✓ Doesn't believe in superlatives
- ✓ Listens to RADIOHEAD
- ✓ Enjoys Swing Dancing
- ✓ Runs for Fun
- ✓ Likes the idea of Driftwood
- ✓ Looks so darn pretty!

Kerouac

Here I am driving through crowded streets. Shrubs, trash, cement, and buildings as far as the eyes can see. People are everywhere, too. Some seem to be going nowhere in particular and others can't stand the wait. And here I am with that hollow, empty, and lonely but in-the-middle-of-it-all feeling. And I'm wondering, no, I'm longing, to be the (last) only person on this planet. I'm dreamin' of inconceivable peace and calm. The only thing is I'm frightened to be alone, thinking alone. And as I turn left up the hill I pass a cemetery so green it's alive. I don't think it knows that it's supposed to die. And then I move on zipping by the dry cleaners and stop at the light by the DQ. It's tempting, but I put it off. I got things to do and people to see, but I forget all that when I notice a beautiful baby, just sittin' there by herself with no shoes. So now my heart starts to accelerate, and I am intrigued to no end. Everything's out the window except lost opportunities. I turn the corner, pull over; it's time for a dip cone. I cross the street feigning oblivion and the not noticing her not noticing me thing. I hop into line and end up with a Pepsi—guess I'm going to be thirsty. Like a failed mission I have fallen to Earth and step back into the crosswalk. But lo! Courage overtakes me. I turn and pop the lid off my drink and head towards the trash where she is sitting. He shoots, he scores! And now I exclaim in a general and raised voice, "How ya doin'?"

She moves slowly on dry land.

I'm lying here and it is nearly 1 A.M. I'm almost fully awake 'cause I got two million things whiz-bangin' through my mind. I guess what has me most riled-up at this moment is the media followed closely by the human predatory nature which I believe is an experiment millions of years since gone bad. So with this defective DNA I settle into an evening of weightlifting and lusting for a girl who can't seem to find it in her genetic code to attack mine. Even worse is that my stuff is all over hers. And then some reason or logic circuit in my head 'clicks on' (cued by the trains outside my window). All this shorts my feelings, but I'm still a little miffed about the virginity thing, and that neither my friends nor anyone else seem to have any idea of the significance of love in a sexual encounter. Then when I finally clear my mind the late news show is all about violence as it pertains to rape. Now I'm petrified. Why are we such a sick species? [I fortify myself completely. Problem: with such definite boundaries, no one gets in.] Who do you like better, the locals or the popular leaders? I have turned this thing over and over, but still I am no wiser.

Three Nights

1

It's cold and I am running solo through the dark woods. My mind is moving towards clarity, my head is pointed downward. Such a strange thing is a shadow cast by the moon. It does not concern me long, for my thoughts turn quickly to my blue woman.

2

Two weeks only and I can hardly remember her. I won't undo the Marshall Tucker sounds and pretty girl smiles for just anyone. She is different, however. How can a brown-eyed girl make me so blue?

3

Xerxes Largo, a chocolate drink box, and a call from Dave do so much to calm this insipid dreaming. Drugs couldn't possibly work better. I know it. A needle never confessed its wonder to me. I stitched my bed spread with her rotten spells cast in casual glances, deep sighs, and overwhelmingly outrageous outbursts. But bitterness is not my drink—the lust is far too sweet.

Welcome to my new day. It is not really so new, but it feels much calmer and is like a forgotten rhythm—a peaceful one.

I am struck by the desire to write wonderful songs. How about something of growing up in Ohio? Or maybe I could put something together about a guy who smiled all the time. But my favorite would have to be about the young lovers and their quiet lust underneath the willow tree.

You got something you just can't hold.
That's love in your heart, but you still feel cold.
Like water in your hand when you squeeze, it's free.
Damn that girl—she ain't too sure about me.

She meets the world on her terms.
Everyday.
In the afternoon come rainy thoughts and impotence.
But I won't let them

touch her with a deep calm voice
All is put to right.
Watch out!
That cat ain't her—she's a stick of dynamite
I trade spices –
cinnamon, nutmeg, chocolate, just to be near her.
She buys them all for a smile,
in her heart a crocodile
Magnets she just don't understand.
She moves so slowly on dry land.

Feel the stream of consciousness.
Sex, money, politics, power steals the soul.
Sell yourself for some fame.
Wide-eyed children know your name.
Don't worry it will all fit on a zip drive.
Do I really believe someone will try and decipher this?
Sleepy.
Broad Road.
Need dry wall mud—least of problems.
Taxes.
Got to read a little before
I sleep.

Swash

This is not a letter. How can I write when I have no chewing gum? For that matter, how can I write while listening to a song about a sweater. (It's not the sweater; it's the harmony, baby!)

I don't know anyone raised on a riverboat, nor anyone named Brunhilda. Of course this doesn't mean I never will. In this river town there is one helluva ripple. I've been here nearly every day of my life, and I still don't know exactly where to go to get what I want.

How would you spend your last Saturday somewhere? Working is a safe bet for the young and insane, but I must warn you not to undertake anything grandiose with one foot on the train. I know this doesn't bother J.Q.P., but if you are insane enough to work down to the last minute, then you must be looking for some closure.

Forget about good days, think of one that sucks. You felt good in the A.M. and then nothing tasted sweet after that first Coke. But it can all turn with the flip of a coin. It must be the fall karma blowing in on that sweet Zephyr. (I wish Zephyr rhymed with Sarsaparilla.)

Sometimes you can't escape Bill and his vicious source code (unless you're the type who wouldn't spend your last Saturday at work). But oh my sweet luck! This week I had a little brown-eyed, blushing Serendipity waiting for me. I can't spell it but it rhymes with tangerine.

I can close my eyes easily tonight. I won't be dreaming about this literary debacle, but of myself standing naked in the park, singing my favorite song, and hurling my favorite four letter words at the hecklers.

Stone Mountain

I rode the sky lift to the top of Stone Mountain. Admittedly the whole experience was not true to my expectations. The heights terrified me. Dangling helplessly from a cable in an aluminum box with thirty other people only intensified the panic. I grasped the rail firmly, and marveled at the four children next to me giggling as we ascended more than four thousand feet up the ominous mountain. (*Aren't little kids supposed to be timid, especially of new and grandiose things?*)

Atop the largest piece of exposed granite in the world I took a breath, and then started taking in all the activity. Americans and foreign visitors alike were engaged in various activities. Some explored the rock and others sat alone. While most milled about in the cool autumn breeze, the lovers sought small formations of wind-blown granite for privacy. Even if they were not alone they pretended to be.

While I strolled about the top, a thought occurred to me: who of this Earth would not wish to walk along the summit of a mountain on a beautiful day such as this? The vista seemed endless. Stone Mountain Park, an astonishing creation, is a wonderland of capitalism, in the same vein as Disneyland. Despite the contrived modernism of the park, after only an hour or so I am defeated and utterly enchanted.

As I write these words, a bee has come to rest on my yellow pad and crawling along the granite is an orange butterfly. To the west is downtown Atlanta. It is shrouded in hazy pollution. The clouds stretch endlessly beneath the perfect afternoon sun. And just maybe it is a little reassuring to have the stalwart figures of Stonewall, Lee, and Davis rolling out beneath me, keeping this rock from crumbling.

Below the giant relief of the Confederate heroes stretches a park and short path. Etched in the stones is information concerning the secession of states from the Union, their admission to the Confederacy, and their subsequent readmission to the Union. In less than an hour I've learned so much. But even more interesting to me are the many quotes from the grandest figures of American history. Never doubt the ability of humans to stir emotions and send a young man to battle with such words as honor, equality, virtue, morality, necessity, glory, integrity, principle, opportunity, promise, duty, liberty, prosperity, compassion, and obligation. In all these rocks not one occurrence of the word "love." I did, however, glimpse a "love" or two in the graffiti covering many of the stones located alongside the path down Stone Mountain.

Don't get me wrong, Stone Mountain is a great place. Here Americans rejoice, but other than listless lovers on the rocks, it does not evoke the spirit of life intrinsic in nature and the earth. At Stone Mountain you will only find your national pride and perhaps a great Fourth of July toast. I anticipated a little more solace as I searched for a place to ponder what I must do for the woman I hold dear to regard me as highly as she does Robert E. Lee. I guess I don't quite understand it, at least not one hundred percent. (*Somebody poured asphalt in the wind hollows of the rock!*)

Daydream

She was my wife in another life. Or perhaps it was the other way around. Regardless, I can see us on green rolling plains the farmer and the horse lover. There are no children, but everything is bursting with life. Clouds roll across the skies with intermittent breaks of sunshine. The stones, the flowers, and the animals are all just a little damp as the Earth in this place is juicy and bursting with life's sustaining waters. The nights and mornings are cool but give way to warmer days. This is it: the beginning and the end. The world has only these dimensions: green, mist, and lovers.

Why must I castrate myself to achieve emotional impotence? I cannot pretend or be a part-time anything. Am I a modern warrior in the business trenches, or am I a passionate lover and writer of verse? It must be one or the other. I know what I'd rather be, but I won't let me. I'm afraid to fill that void. That VOID! (I tell myself that no one feels the same, nobody would be interested in the stuff I write.)

Fuck it all! I never would, never could. I don't believe it when someone claims indifference. If you have no feeling you are dead. But not dead as a rock is dead; a rock is the history of this earth and as such is alive.

No. A dead person, when still breathing, is a pathetic thing. How sad it is to those alive to see someone without hope, missing all the sensations like sand between the toes and cinnamon beneath the nose. How strange it is that we the living should be envious! You fucking lifeless bastards! You only exist to magnify our negative emotions. We don't even see you when we are passionately in love. (On a sunny day I forget about the Henry Millers of this world.)

So here I am at the brink of love with a woman I know completely and not at all. She has a home 17,000 miles away *as the crow flies*. (All these seductresses in my own nefarious land, and I am utterly mad for a foreigner.)

She is not the only one ever to get me, but so far she is closer to the eternal purchase than any other lady has ever been. All this said it is the same chipped tooth. My stomach hurts, my heart sinks, and overall I am lousy. God help those who must tolerate me!

Oh, how I need to dance! Demons in the walls come let me feel your techno beats in a trance-like oblivion! Show me the pale shadows of your faces as I cross the sea of anonymity, careful only to touch those with a slight pulse. I can smell the stench of the living dead and only the music can hold me. I want her. Eventually we are thrown to the street.

It is the same feeling for me. I want her so badly but the gods conspire against me. How can tomorrow follow this midnight of the soul? Nothing will save me. I will drown in a sea of tears, though not one shed. Instead they are suffocating me from the inside. Forgetting my feelings works, that's all. How? Why I get lost in work, that's how. I join the undead. There is no ritual. Just stop doing that which makes you live—*feel.*

The neo-classical human of impeccable virtue is particularly susceptible. Finding him is like finding a four-leaf clover. When found, the urge to pick him is overwhelming. Leave him in the earth!

I will not die but perforce! Take me from this Earth and put me on the pavement of a dark, dripping metropolis. I can tolerate the gargoyles and buzzards circling in anticipation. The stone weariness makes me harder but I can't fight the feeling. Thank goodness it is too late for me. In this brave new world I will have peace; I will have love; I will have solitude.

I can wait, wait happily without fear or worry. I want her. She knows that. Should the dead conspire to keep us apart, my goddess will surely appear in another shape and form. And this time we will have children.

War Love Letter (Dear Helen)

I write to you in utter desperation and need. You must have an inkling of what I am about to say. Yet for as long as you have known, your silence mocks my heavy heart. I wait calmly and patiently, appearing the pillar of strength and virtue. (That is what you want, right? You need to feel safe and protected. You want someone who can shield you from the mixed sensations of life.) In reality I am a weir of emotion straining to control myself.

With your last letter came the orders that sent a thousand men to their death. Unspeakable horrors abound. For your beauty and the stewardship of your love a war is being fought.

You are not a victim in this conflagration, but your innocence is noted. How could you know your blushing smile would send the mighty Ares to his chariot? Who would have thought your kind heart with its soulful discourses and the morning mist of your kiss would be so potent?

I am helpless to stop the fighting. My job is to contain it and one day to draft an accord. Complete and total dominance by one side seems unlikely. Rather a stalemate will ensue and the spoils will be divided, you among them. Then all will realize your frailty. As always you will be cherished, but as disillusionment grows among the ranks, you will be forced to withdraw.

Step forward now. End this struggle. Tell me, tell me, tell me... I shall turn these arms into a monument of humankind. So long as the sun leaps into the morning sky, so long as the moon calls the tides, so long will I love and cherish you.

Confession

Nail bitin' but the hands don't look too shabby. On the wrist is wet leather and what remains of the bamboo strap. He doesn't feel like doing this except when he's in love. Actually, he's never been in love—lust mostly. (The NASA pen is working furiously now!) And the one time he broke a girl's heart still causes that sinking feeling and a quiet rage. He was barely a man and not in love. She, a handsome and generally kind-hearted woman, was never idle in searching…a man always on her horizon. She worked in the forest setting traps. I don't think she meant to keep him, but sometimes you're not sure what you've caught. He was stunned, and in idle times a willing captive. Call her Dido, for there was no chance of togetherness. Let the similarities stop there. He so badly wanted to feel something. She longed for the longing of a man. No sooner than a beginning's end they parted. Her punishment was a scorned love. His punishment a shame turned inward and aimless searching.

True Desires

It seems to me that we as people are fondest of that which we cannot have, or rather cannot come by so easily. Often the "pie in the sky" is prosperity, but capitalism has bastardized this elusive desire and now it has become greed. In fact there is little in this world we (Americans) cannot pursue in the utter certainty we shall succeed in obtaining it. Still, quite the opposite has come true as of late. We obsess in our wealth and are easily overcome by it. We have "too much of a good thing."

Good people are lost each day. It is not easy to decipher what you want and what you really need. I know. Many of us keep the answer in the darkest recesses of our mind. Alone with thought we are virtuous and free about our true desires. Like sparks, life triggers the emotions inherent in us. That accountant never wanted anything more than to be the leader of a marching band (*too silly, no money in that!*). That bus driver really, really wanted to be a law professor (*no self-assurance or family support!*). This politician wants to be a hairdresser (*freedom must be an illusion!*). And so it goes.

I make no bones about it. The truth for me lies close to the surface. Again, it seems, no one dares ask another for the truth in desires. I hold it close, but dig ever so slightly and you will see it all. I desire to be a writer, a poet, a philosopher, a man who makes others think, smile, and cry. And though I can scarcely imagine a sweeter life, all this I would gladly trade for the love of one woman. (I am American; must I sacrifice anything?) Work as a mole in an office my whole life, I could, for that love of mine. Of course I would never see it beneath me to stoop to the earth to gather the food we eat. If she bids it, I will do it.

I plan to get off with a lighter sentence, and with equal depth of love. Nonetheless, that is my true desire: true love. Tonight as I type this I look down at my body. It is sore as I am working hard to restore the strength and shape so recently lost. My body fights wars on many fronts, against many foes. I appreciate this. My mind must help. And so it shall.

Augustinian Dialogue

"Were your other women prettier than I am?"

"You know there weren't many. Only one really."

"Well, her?"

"You must know?"

"I must."

"Yes."

"How so?"

"She was more beautiful in a reality whose existence I no longer recognize. You, fair lady, make me whole. Your looks are so becoming that the mere sight of you softens all rough edges."

"How can that be? You said she was prettier."

"True, but I wouldn't recognize her should I meet her in a crowd. For all I know her face is everywhere, and has graced the pages of thousands of magazines…or even daily flashes across millions of screens.

"Sure, she was prettier. Her eyes were bluer, her hair was blonder, and her skin was darker. But you, you my darling, for all your inconsistencies and 'un-pretty' qualities, you are the more real to me. In your eyes I see every color. In your hair I find waves of soft silk. Your touch is the electric of splitting atoms.

"You are infinite, infinitely mine. Beauty is such a narrow concept that she was, or perhaps is, the more of it. The possibility within you, and the thrill of knowing not knowing, is my love for you."

…

"Give me a second."

"Why?"

"I think I might cry."

"Then why are you smiling?"

"Because I never know what you're going to say."

Twilight

I think you're in the right, and still I understand the plight of the romantic. Ya' know there is this me that is rough around the edges. I've got this idea that I'm somewhere out on the plains. The sky stretches forever in a blue-gray-yellow twilight. The land is a fading dark green. I'm weary. The only thing holding me up is my old pair of jeans and my work boots. I stride confidently and rub my chin. (Which is rougher my hand or my face?) I walk into a roadside diner. There are a few people scattered about the place and the jukebox is playing "Moonwalker" by Santos and Johnny. I sit quietly at the counter. I hate coffee, but I order one 'cause I can't get rid of the salty taste in my mouth. Overcome with the haste of hunger, I hardly taste my dinner. For dessert I order a piece of pie and look dreamily past the old waitress. I'm tryin' to remember a time when she was beautiful and would've broken my heart. I stretch my arms quietly and leave far too much for a tip. I'm outta here, don't know if I'll be back.

I get into my old pickup and drive until I catch up to the horizon. Everywhere stand tall buildings in asphalt furrows. There is not a speck of dust on me now. I open the car door and step onto the black, damp street. A horn startles me and I look upward, searching for the sun. At the top of the stairs I turn around and see my car with lights flashing. I brace myself with a tug on my jacket and walk through the colossal columns and into the bank. The resemblance to a sarcophagus is uncanny. The shining marble floors echo with each step. Some guy with a gun and blue shirt eyeballs me. I curse his ignorance, amuse myself with the thought of giving him a hug, and join the line. My mind drifts to the mother of pearl clouds I saw in the desert and I want to buy them, or even just a puff of them, and give them to my lover. "Can I help you? Sir?" I'm standing across from a black woman. Her stare is absent. Her nameplate reads "Julia Brookes." I'm not sure if the soiled check or my suit surprises her more. "Just a moment, sir." She types furiously and then counts out $500. "Have a nice day," she says. "You, too, Julia." But I forget to wink.

December 2000

The loneliness returned as quickly as it departed. It swept over me like the snow that blanketed Chicago two days ago. Only time would diminish this burden (and the determination to fill the void in my life).

Why does flying fill me with such inescapable sadness? The gentleman from Idaho sitting next to me on the way to Salt Lake City awakened romantic yearnings of the imagined West of yesteryear. You know what I'm talking about—the snow swept mountains and the flowered plains all unspoiled by man's presence and so far removed from the problems of our reality?

The girl in front of me pierced my heart with a blade of lust. Her flawless complexion, her softly defined profile, her lush flowing hair, and her abstract desires stung me with a primeval longing to touch, caress and kiss. But in her eyes was a void as dark as her leather jacket and as distant as the ground beneath us.

Now I am on the last leg of my lonely journey home. At last! But it is not over—not the journey, not the work, not even the yearning. The other day, when it was snowing in Chicago, I sat outside the downtown post office watching the snow from the warmth of my car. (Even the city is quiet when the snow is falling.) Inside of me was the din of techno music churning from the speakers. The poetry of the moment did not escape me.

Trail

I stumbled down the canyon wash as though I were a drunk on Vine Street. Every twisted root was a rattlesnake and every charred log a sleeping black bear. I could hardly imagine how water might find its way on this arid path.

We (*my thoughts and I*) went on that way for about an hour and a half. At last I came to the narrow pass where the Devil supposedly resides. I proceeded cautiously down the stone corridor imagining an ambush by U.S. Cavalry or some ragged frontiersmen forgotten in time. About halfway through I peered up from the grassy floor, my eyes tracking the towering rocks to the thin blue band of sky. At this moment I realized I was standing in the birth canal of the West Texas Mountains.

The realization was heavy, so I stopped there for a moment. I glanced down at my watch. I didn't know it then, but my faithful timepiece was nearing the end of its usefulness. Twelve noon, the time I promised myself I'd find a suitable spot to kick back, enjoy some water, and perhaps a snack. But the other side of this pass was beckoning me.

After thirty or so more yards I was on the far side of the canyon and alone in the shade. Right in front of me stood a small pole, on top of which a plaque was mounted. "End of Trail," it read. I chuckled and looked around. It seemed to me that I might decide for myself if this was the end. For as far as the eye could see the rocks continued in much the same fashion as they had for the last several miles. The only item missing was those neatly stacked rocks left at regular intervals by a ranger or Good Samaritan hiker to assure those without a keen sense of direction that they were not yet lost.

I found a nice comfortable rock to settle upon. It was in the shade, but I had no choice in the matter. It was the logical place, about ten feet from the sign indicating I had come to the end of the trail. So I sat quietly enjoying some water and peanut M&Ms.

I don't exactly recall my idle thoughts on that rock, but I do remember my mind being abuzz with romantic imaginings of days long gone when Texas was no more than a whisper in the western wind. I reminded myself, "You're here looking for Spring. You may have to look a little deeper, that's all."

"Would you mind keepin' it down over there?" the sign asked.

The sign spoke!

I took a deep breath, stood up, and peered over and around the rocks. A sweat stain was left where I was sitting.

"Keep what down?" I laughed out loud.

"The noise, the noise coming from your head. I haven't heard this much gibberish from one person since that Fred Savage kid hiked up here."

The sign just stood there.

"Don't just look at me. Say something!" he cried. (I say he because he sounded just like a guy from New Jersey named Marty.)

Believe it or not words come easy when you're talking to a sign. "What's your name?" I asked.

"Red Star. Red Star Cleveland," replied the sign. "Don't tell me yours. I bet you're William the Conqueror."

"You've got me pegged all wrong Red."

"Red Star!"

"I'm sorry, Red Star. Weren't you listening to what I was thinking?"

"Listening?! It sounded like a third grade music class. What the hell have you got going on in there?"

"Lots of stuff, but mostly romantic, poetic, listless imaginings."

"I thought I might've heard an angel singing," he snapped.

"Listen Red," I said.

"Red Star!"

"Pardon, I meant Red Star. I've never really talked to a sign before. What gives?"

"Yeah? Well I don't talk to many people either. Most can't even hear me. You just sorta looked lonely and that gray matter between your ears was making so much goddamned racket I just couldn't sleep."

"My apologies, Red Star. I came here to find peace of mind in the blossoming Spring. It's kinda strange how I run into you here at the end of the trail."

"Glad to oblige. You know there are worse places to be if you're a sign."

"Tell me about it," I said.

"I knew a couple of other signs before they put me up here, but they were mostly bathroom signs. Ya know, like 'Please Flush,' 'Put Trash In Its Place,' and my favorite: 'Sanitized For Your Safety.' Oh boy, she was a peach!"

An awkward silence followed this last exchange.

"So what exactly brings you here?" Red Star asked.

"Happiness."

"Happiness?"

"That's right, I'm looking for happiness."

"Have you found it?" the sign asked sincerely.

"In small bits and pieces. But I feel even if I'm not happy more often, I should at least enjoy my days a little more."

"You don't enjoy your life?" the sign coaxed.

"No. It is hard for me to say that, but it's true. I have things I look forward to—a day here or there; you know, traveling, or a visit with a friend. But day in and day out I feel depressed.

"I don't know," said the sign. "I've met a lot of people while posing for lots of pictures. Of 'em all you're one of a very few who seems to have a really good shot at happiness."

"How can you tell?"

"'Cause you know you're not happy and 'cause I think you have a good idea what will make you happy. Most people that end up here beside me don't realize whether they're happy or not. They're all distracted, lost in this world. Hell, most don't even say 'Hello' when I do talk to them!"

"Red Star, I've heard it said that knowledge comes but wisdom lingers. How did you get to be so wise?"

"I'm a sign," he chirped in that conceited New Jersey accent.

I slowly put my belongings back into my pack while reflecting on the words of Red Star. I didn't feel self-conscious in any way because I was certain Red Star had seen it all before. You know what I'm talking about—hiker reaches the end of the trail, looks around, enjoys a drink and heads back.

"Don't go if there's something else bothering you. I've got a long afternoon ahead and tomorrow's Monday. I may not see anyone until next weekend."

I laughed. "There's always the mule deer."

Red Star, quite seriously, replied, "There is one who's kinda cute. She doesn't come by often, but if she were to stop by right now I'd pretend you don't even exist."

I laughed again incredulously, and then pondered his words for a moment. Before even realizing it I blurted out, "What ever could exist between you and a deer?"

"My searching friend, happiness, like all things, is a perception. It exists within you."

So certain was his reply, I sat stupefied.

"Red Star, what do you mean a perception? I have books on my shelf I won't read because I don't understand them. Is this a matter of perception?"

"Absolutely. It is common belief we must react to our environment rather than meet it or exist within it."

"I don't follow."

"In football, if the defense shifts to the right and you're carrying the ball, then you cut left. You react. But in baseball if you're playing catcher and a runner is heading home, you'd better be there to meet him. In one situation you avoid, in the other you engage."

"And your meaning?"

"My meaning, lone hiker, is that the world exists within you. Me, the mule deer, and your happiness is a part of this. It is all as real as these rocks that surround us. But at the same time it is your perception or interpretation of the intelligence that surrounds us all."

"I'm overwhelmed."

"Am I a sign or intelligence expressed as wood and plastic?"

"Am I an intelligent expression of flesh and bone?"

"That I cannot answer."

"You're really screwing with my head Red."

"Red Star! And you've missed the point here. Your perception is taking over."

"Right."

"Take a drink and relax for a moment."

"My mind is exhausted."

"Yeah, well, how do you think I feel sittin' out here half-baked every day in the sun?"

"How long have you been here?"

"Long enough to have met all the mule deer in the park and too many scorpions."

I took a deep breath before continuing and on the exhale I spoke my piece. "So how do I escape my perceptions?"

"Look, I don't have all the answers," he said in a rather humble tone. "But your goal shouldn't be to escape your perceptions, only to alter them a little. Change comes slowly; just ask these mountains."

"I might," I muttered under my breath.

"It's impossible for you to escape this reality. Your mind won't tolerate it. But as things evolve, subsequent generations will not hold the same truths as we do, nor will they be hindered by our limits."

"I'm not so optimistic, Red Star."

"That doesn't really matter. But this shouldn't be depressing. There is no way for us to conceptualize the world as it really is. Therefore we try to encapsulate the moment. There is no right or wrong."

"You've taken me to the edge. I want to wrap my mind around it all, but then I see the abyss and my breath becomes shallow while my heart sinks."

"Don't separate yourself from it all. You, me, and the scorpions are all part of the infinite possibility."

"You're a damn talking sign, Red Star!"

"That is what your senses tell you. But maybe we are one and the same: intelligence, albeit expressed differently."

I sat there without speaking for what seemed like forever. The sun was now turning toward its downward arc. Red Star became less animated and I almost lost him, as you might lose the image in one of those magic eye prints sold at the mall.

Admittedly I liked what Red Star had to say. My own beliefs and perceptions had taken me only so far. I was far too myopic in my views. When I got to the precipice I had seen only entropy and infinite chaos. Now a sign that read "End of Trail" had calmed my mind like a fun diversion, but without the loss of consciousness.

"It is time for me to go, Red Star."

"Well I must say it has been a pleasure. Not too many folks make it this far up the canyon, and even fewer have anything meaningful to say. Hell, some even shove their tired asses right up in front of me."

"Thank you for the enlightenment. You have opened my eyes and now I must unlearn some things in order to move forward," I said smiling.

"Before you go would you mind pouring a little of your water on my face? It gets kind of dusty out here and I don't expect much moisture until next winter."

"You betcha, Red."

"Red Star!"

I met some other hikers on the way back through the canyon. While they all seemed quite friendly I didn't tell them about Red Star or the things he shared with me. I figured they might meet him without my help, or they may just have to find their way elsewhere. Anything's possible.

Reinventing the B:Drive

Saturday, only two weeks ago, I stepped off the plane and into her arms. I think she was expecting much more, but what she got was a trembling boy full of thought, a weir of emotions. In our embrace she could feel the thumping in my chest. (A better writer would have me come ashore, reminiscent of General MacArthur, with a flower in hand and the words: "This virtuous woman shall be taken, and I am the man to do it," reverberating from my lips.)

And so began my strange odyssey into life, love, and sex. It is astonishing what fear can do for people—not too much though—just more than is necessary. Fear is an easy emotion, much like loneliness. (With fear and loneliness it is always best to have a little patience.)

In the coming hours the awkwardness would wane but not her beauty. To know someone and to appreciate them from a distance is much different than having them in your pocket. To be fair to her I don't know women, and quite possibly I am a fool. My mind was so completely open that day I couldn't possibly escape its reaches. (How would you feel if you looked into someone's eyes and saw a room the size of a black hole sparsely decorated with a couple of ideas, thoughts, and colorless feelings?)

We kissed, but we talked more, and without real depth. It was like being in a city of the future where it is difficult to concentrate. In the preceding weeks she had worked tirelessly to pry me open, and when her wandering parakeet finally arrived, with equal effort she labored to stem the flood of my emotions.

Our phone calls were deep, relaxing, and occasionally funny; the emails, too. But where were those feelings in Chicago? I felt like the poet who had drowned while trying to kiss the moon in the water. What to do? What could we do? Our two worlds were on a windy city collision course. Accordingly we abandoned whiskey in favor of champagne and its misty promises. In doing so we were able to find a peculiar ecstasy on Sunday.

When it comes to women I am always a gentlemen, but boastfully admit there are exceptions. Unfortunately this weekend was not one of those occasions. I speculate when I say, much to her chagrin.

We took solace in our physical compatibility. In this arena I was little more than a pupil. Even in my confusion I must have done something right, for as the chasm opened between us so too developed an understanding that melted the bronze from my heart.

Bidding her farewell at that same airport where she rescued me was difficult only because we had figured out a connection. Our chance encounter months ago had now produced a rainbow. From her light came a physical connection which heretofore I had mistakenly regarded with the reverence of religion. And just maybe my raindrops surprised her a little because I don't think she was ever allowed to feel the tiny sensations in life.

I applaud anyone willing to follow a beckoning love. Yes, I know these are the words of a hyper-romantic, but that is part of me. If two worlds are able to become one, then you must never take the time to make up your mind about people.

Bitter at my love.

I cannot believe what I am relating is my own story. This cannot be my life. But it is, and it pains me. I never thought I would grow tired of the warm body next to me. I remember when it was so new and so nearly overwhelming. To hold her was to live. And now…now she is poisoning my heart.

Truthfully she hasn't changed in the least. Her beauty is still evident in her face, her body, and her grace in these difficult times. The metamorphosis is within me.

Oh how I loathe this woman! Just breathing the same vapid air as her sickens me. I can barely stand the existence of our child, let alone fathom the idea of sleeping next to her.

I know there is no rationale for my feelings. Yes, I am afflicted with a horrendous disease. If the devil lives, it is in my cells.

I almost recall our blissful happiness, but it fades into dark at the very sight of our monstrous offspring. Our love was perfect, but my seed was sown in a demon valley. Together we produced a horrendous living thing that will not die but feeds on, nay devours, our once boundless love.

Now it is nearly gone. I blame her, my wife. How could she let such a creature grow inside her? Certainly I am not responsible for our hideous spawn.

Soon I will be no more, but not before the child takes all that I have. Dreams of the future have become nightmares of apocalyptic landscapes swept in human ashes. There was a time I counted myself fortunate, for not every man marries his true love. Yet such permanent ecstasy is not the privilege of a mortal man.

Reflections on a Tragedy

I haven't been on the verge of tears so often since I was a child. My heart is torn, but it is a good thing. How can this be? What of those who lost their lives, their friends, and their family members? I know not what to say to assuage their anger, nor to relieve their pain. Yet today I live, where yesterday I existed. Feelings I thought lost but for the occasional romantic poem have surfaced like the adrenaline that surged within my veins as an adolescent. As the smoke cleared on the ruination of our society, the brilliance of life shone anew.

Some people like this country for what it has given them; others love it for the myth and power. But I love it for what it is: the grandest microcosm of all the world's diversity. Despite the internal divisiveness, at odd hours of crisis, the many become one.

Her

It is not as warm tonight and still the fire within, best described as longing, waxes and wanes with every beat of my heart. A beautiful woman on the street or at the gym is like a gust of wind that sends sparks throughout my body. Yet there is but one woman who is my constant, the burning ember that keeps my heart aglow. Her eyes betray her innocence, and bespeak an ageless sorcery. Though I am no more than a speck of dust in these transoceanic winds, I relish the burning, the dire yearning, as though it were hell's fury.

We've started across that line, and the most important thing is for me to remain myself.

I recall our first kiss for its softness, but visually I remember a slide show as I blinked for long intervals. Her nose, her teeth, her bottom lip, my lips, her top lip…slow, easy, soft, natural, memorable.

Transcription

I think I'm a bit closer to her and to understanding her. I felt a little self-pity this evening when she didn't call me back as soon as I expected. But when she did I became tender. At least that's how she made me feel. For some strange reason she came across the line even more feminine, more womanly, than I can ever remember. This alone caused a yearning within me, the likes of which I haven't felt for a long, long time. Don't let it frighten you, but it is so powerful that I want to consume her, or in other words, make her a part of me.

Forsaken among a patch of red berries.
I'm all stressed again and for no good reason. Unless not wanting to waste your life doing something you don't enjoy has some merit. I shouldn't complain because I do like some of it, and I'm sure I can make it fun. My goal is to be professional (the most) and laugh with my co-workers.

Being able to articulate how I feel is a great relief.
The last couple of days must have been extremely difficult for her. After our kiss I was a bit incredulous, perhaps to the point of being suspect. I truly wondered what had softened her heart to my advances. (Was it time? Experience? Fear?) Yet she must have been even more overwhelmed by it. The thought, "What have I done?" must have entered her mind. So for a couple of days she has had to face the prospect of our next meeting and that moment when I would want to kiss her again.

I am back in the fold.
I wish I could just go to sleep the way I did when I was a kid. But I want to see how it will all work out: the negotiations, the infrastructure, this season, and most of all this life.

Thus are the whims of the rich.
I'm just plain tired. My struggle is far less important than anything even a child could imagine—or is it? Every day I stave off savage

attacks on my soul. I am victorious so long as there is something worth fighting for.

I think some people—maybe most—feel the presence of something intangible and powerful in their lives. They try to define and name this feeling. God, Allah, Yahweh, Buddha, and Jesus are but a few examples. A much smaller group of people simply revels in this feeling. Some ignore it or are incapable of feeling it.

Talk to me.

"You know I think you are a fool."

"Have you run out of kind words?" she replied.

"Almost. But my meaning is not harsh. I am sad because you are a fool. I don't know what to think of myself for adoring a fool."

(Long pause.)

"I suspected my words would elicit only silence. What goes on in your mind? You speak of the Phantom and how he urges Christine to join him in a new life. Am I the fool?"

What I should have done.

I should have reassured her. I should have pulled her close and told her not to worry, that I would be there. I should have kissed her tenderly and held her close. If I wanted her to be at ease I should have told her I know how she feels. Nobody should fear a burgeoning relationship.

All business…

I feel like if I work hard everything else will fall into place. I can't worry about how each individual behaves. For me, the most important things are sanity and my health. Sanity comes from having a life, and health from this sanity. I know if we communicate well, all will fall into place.

In the belly…

I know why we ignore the voice of reason. When I hear Led Zeppelin sing how she shook him all night long, I understand. And this is the same group that will leave her where the guitar is played.

POETRY

FIRST COLLECTION:
1992—1995

A Poem

"Who are you?" she pled.
"Does it matter?" he said.
"Can you see me?" asked she.
"In a manner of speaking," said he.
'Do you love me?" whispered she.
"Only when I touch you," mumbled he.
"Why do you treat me so?" she cried.
"I don't know," he lied.

Alone

My shoulders are young, and they are broad.
But they cannot bear what all of us share.
Come, ease my loneliness…

Bury the Dead

Beautiful cemetery so green and alive,
your ancient mysteries I cannot contrive.
Enduring monuments rise up so high,
have you not forgotten you're supposed to die?

CAVEAT

When life tears my soul a gapin' hole,
I often put pen to paper.

And what I write, a horrendous sight,
seems to be romantic garbage.

Yet if you look beyond the love-sick song,
there is plenty of hidden meaning.

So if you read my work, don't go berserk,
and laugh or cry exceedingly.

Cryptic Bursts II

Life: To know your own mortality and that you are part of something greater.

To be granted physical eternity would be a curse.

Myths allow us to open a mysterious realm.

In my wake I leave your body, preferring only your soul to keep.

He reached into the sky and handed her a star.

She dipped her hand into the sea and gave him life.

It all began innocently enough.

My body left long before. My soul remained forevermore.

The dead live in the blood of the living.

Few things scare me so, as those I do not know.

I am the beast who upon life does feast.

There is something about a girl who sings.

There is no written or spoken language in the world that can adequately express feelings.

We are going to find our future in our distant past.

I don't want to start a movement. I want to end one.

Dedication

I write to no one person but my lover;
where she is I cannot discover.

Descartes

The man about whom I write
was trapped in an age-old fight.
In life he found little meaning,
yet his fate kept intervening.
It sought to teach him love,
a concept he viewed from above.
Instead he turned to his learning,
but it only increased his yearning.

Over time the truth became clear.
However it only increased his fear.
For what he realized was this:

Life is only bliss,
And somewhere between animal and artificial is man…

"Great"

The days are long but I see her clearly.
I wonder if she knows I want her near me.
The sun rises, the sun sets;
she wakes thinking, and in sleep forgets.

On certain mornings it is her form I behold,
yet it is her soul that warms my cold.
The sun rises, the sun sets;
she wakes thinking, and in sleep forgets.

Scarred by eternity I pass her by,
concealing vulnerabilities I would deny.
The sun rises, the sun sets;
she wakes thinking, and in sleep forgets.

Behold her power to crush the darkness,
her hand extended in naked starkness.
The sun rises, the sun sets;
she wakes thinking, and in sleep forgets.

Our touch glows in the bleakest night.
love transcends all if not put to flight.
Joined as one in age-old repair;
we learn as much as we are willing to share.

The sun rises, the sun sets;
she dwells within me, in her I forget.

Gothic Love

The night both clear and cold,
did wax of stories often told.
The sanctuary stood still and dim,
as its bell tolled a perilous hymn.

A beautiful lady walked far from sight
avoiding paths of flooding light.
Within her darkness a tear did fly,
filled with a love unwilling to die.
For it is a terrible, terrible thing to adore
that which death can touch forevermore.

Now the beast swooped down on her as if the wind,
and ravaged her love with a savage grin.
He cut so deep he touched her heart,
but found true love he could not tear apart.

"Why do you hurt me so?" she cried,
"can you not see the pain I hold inside?"
"What I see is deep, dark despair,
that ages ago I, too, did share.
Come with me; you must surrender.
I know a place where love is tender."

She looked into his wild eyes
and saw the truth only a fool denies.
Off they went to the land of the undead,
where as king and queen they made their bed.

Incrimination

Sometimes I feel so volatile,
I could kill…kill with a smile.

It Should Be So Easy

He resides on your surface;
I penetrate deep.
He desires you today,
I want you to keep.

Join Us!

Today we opened a myth and grabbed the helm.
Suddenly we were in a mysterious realm.
Upon this strange sea, our conscience was set free,
and the mist hid nothing but you and me.

As we sailed we witnessed the miracle of birth,
and knew this realm was much like Earth.
We beheld the agony of violent death
as an Amazon warrior gasped her last breath.

Hercules appeared on the starboard side,
his strength rippling in the morning tide.
Across the bow the figure of Helen shone,
such beauty mortal man had never known.

Over the masthead flew a vision of love,
soaring ever so calmly was God's white dove.
But the Ancient Mariner saw it as did we,
and wounded it with an arrow from the sacred tree.

Undaunted we plunged into deeper waters
until the ship hit empty coffers.
Each glistening box displayed a crafted name,
a man or woman of eternal fame.

You begged me to read the names aloud,
so I started with the man of infamous shroud.
"Jesus," I read, but could not continue,
for we shuddered in the cold of this sinister venue.

"No more," I said, "I've seen mine,
"and I don't want to be part of this floating shrine.
"Let us plot a brand new course,
"one in which all people and all things are of an equal force."

"Spread immortality as if it were free,
"but add to it this one decree:
"the violators will suffer Ahab's fate,
"in this mythological world of love and hate."

"However, those who do willingly abide,
"we shall escort to the triple divide,
"where water flows along three paths,
"and there are no such things as epitaphs."

You pressed your lips against mine,
and the pact was sealed with approval divine.
The wind then blew in our direction
as we sailed on carrying infinite perfection.

Memorandum #1

When you see me
remember, it's the little things.

When you hear me
remember, it's the little things.

When you court me
remember, it's the little things.

When you kiss me
remember, it's the little things.

When you smile at me
remember, it's the little things.

When you receive me
remember, it's the little things.

When you bury me
remember, it was the little things
(that made our relationship so special).

OBTHE1

"Where are you?" she said.
"Oh, but does it matter?" he said.
"In a manner of speaking," gasped she.
"Well then I'm peeping," laughed he.
"But you mustn't," whispered she.
"And why not?" implored he.
"Your eyes burn so deep," trembled she.
"That's because I love you," declared he.

She Whispers to Me

She is the sea upon which I sail.
She is the way in a world without trails.
She is the moon that makes my skin rise.
She is the black cat with the hunter's eyes.

Everywhere I look she is all that I see,
except for a few others very similar to me.
It frightens me so to blink in her presence,
for I might fall in love with her silky-smooth essence.

Perhaps it scares me even more than it should.
So I stand here alone a tree of hard wood.
Then she sweeps through the forest a warm, gentle breeze.
Still her love blows me down and scatters my leaves.

"No," I call out as the tears come flyin',
"the world is much easier without lovin' and dyin'."
She smiles and whispers to me as only she can,
nods her beautiful head, and touches my hand.

"Be not afraid, I hold within me the light.
"Join your hand with mine and end this old fight."
She wipes away the lone tear from my eye,
creating the land, the lakes, and the sky.

Eternity groans as we unite under the sun,
for it knows the war we have already won.
No longer will the terror of loneliness strike me down,
because it ain't so easy, destiny, to uncrown.

The Fair Life

The shortest day of the year has come round.
It is dark and gloomy and devoid of sound.
I look out the window that faces the east,
checking ever-so-often for my personal beast.

My mind, so weary, moves neither here nor there,
and my morning eyes are transfixed in a stare.
"Lonely," I hear whispered on a far-off tide,
and I see fate grinning, as if me to chide.

What happened last night: good or bad?
In the dark of ignorance I am utterly sad.
Worry not, I say, drop all your cares,
you know very well life is not always fair.

Too Close Years (2 Years Apart)

Ya know I've never been,
but I have to go, to Westminster Abbey.

I want to see the Gothic architecture rise,
that surely meant many a man's demise.

I want to hear the boom of the bells,
and the shrill sound of little girls' yells.

I want to climb the towers in the sky,
and with mixed emotions utter a sigh.

But I also want to see the history of our age,
and implore your help as we turn the page.

For in the evening mist will we be free
to carve a new existence for you and me.

I really, really need to go to Westminster Abbey.

What People Want

What do people want the most?
The Father, the Son, and the Holy Ghost?

I decided to ask a friend.
"They want to know what comes in the end."

No, I thought, that cannot be.
They want the love of all and they want to be free.

"And you," asked my friend.
"Don't you wish to know about the end?"
"Of course not," I replied,
"That belongs to those who died.
"I want the love of people, and fame thereafter.
"For I possess knowledge of the hereafter."

"Think more clearly," came her voice from the heavens.
"You're ever so lucky I carry your sevens.
"Go now and share your life with her,
"and know that with me your fame is secure."

Thus fate smiled upon me.
Forever after I will hold the key.

1996

A.I.

I sit in wonder.
Often.
I wonder about you.
I wonder what will make me laugh tomorrow.
I wonder what makes me mad.
(In my angst I found Zeppelin. What will I do if the levee breaks?)
I wonder why Vegas is the modern Mecca.
So I have this affair with letters.
(Yet nothing seems to improve with ink.)

Walpole tells me that the world is a tragedy to those who feel, but a comedy to others who think—I am on the fence.
I have been across the Continental Divide all the way to the City of Angels where I saw no divinities but the Ocean, who refused to swallow me.
Tolstoy tells the weeping Indian in Santa Fe, if he wants to be happy, be.
(Now he sells his magic and soul on a chain.)
Therefore, I must refute Carlyle's theory that the essence of humor is love and not contempt.
(At least as it now stands.)

Sometimes I get so tired of the hypocrisy, competition, and apparent neutrality that I want to scream.
(Who would care? Who will read this?)
Snarl.
My savage innocence begets a poisonous clarity.

I sit in wonder.
When the sunshine lifts the foggy sadness, it will all have seemed so silly…

(Angst)Where do you want to go today?

Angst-driven outta time,
sick of workin' for nickel and dime.
All fed up and no place to run,
his mind on the end his hand on the gun.

Thinkin' 'bout the deeper things,
temper flares and mood swings.
Life ain't 'bout the money and drugs,
sleepin' with women and cheerin' thugs.
And it ain't 'bout church and a home out beyond.
Don't give me that shit it's time to go on.

Somebody said, and I stooped to listen,
told me that life can be sweet for the kissin'.
The lesson it stuck and grew from within.
ignorance is bliss, mine is ruin.

Emotions are powerful…I feel them all.
Hope springs eternal until the fall.
Believe I won't, or can't, find the meaning.
Statue of Liberty soon will be leaning.

Life outta control nothing to stop it,
bullshit aside who will profit?
Those at the top fall from grace;
those that know shoot into space.

Joy feelin', pain cast aside,
gettin' on the train, headin' outside,
can't wait to see what's happenin' tomorrow,
there's still a chance I may end all the sorrow.

B. Volio

Methinks there is much reason to your rhyme,
yet to merely think hath no place in love.
I am no more in the throes of passion at this juncture in time
then are the clouds in the heavens above.
A man who art in love makes not sweet decisions,
his body oft marred by his delusional visions.

Still the table of life rolls out before me,
and is only part of the continent I must consume.
The question is not love, but be or not be.
Apocalyptic thoughts I must entomb.

Fall 1996

I have seen much, and heard much more still.
Yet many years will pass before I get my fill.
Each morn' rips me from peaceful slumber.
I trip into the world full of sadness and wonder.

Challenges abound for all that I see.
So few stop to simply be free.
They run here and there, not-so-mindless drones.
I understand the plight their vagueness bemoans.

Five years have passed since I let go the plan.
One day this year I awoke a grown man.
My fears and worries I resolved to let go.
No longer would I fear Fate's random deathblow.
So I resolved to see that place hinter,
where nary a snowflake visits in winter.

I know why there, but cannot admit
that it will look different with the same old shit.

Liberty

I believe nothing.
Nothing is so hopeless as this realization, revelation.
I believe nothing.
Where did the seed come from?
I believe in nothing.
This is not true; I believe in myself (at least I used to).
I believe in no one.
Only the people I've met seem real.
I believe not in not knowing.
I believe not in knowing.
Trapped I am until I believe.
Trapped I am until into my life I weave:
Someone…
Something…
Anything…
To believe in…

I only doubt myself because this world exists within me.
I only contemplate this because I am free.

Keeper of the "BE"

Peace comes in the night.
Only then are things put to right.
Yet the revealing day is sure to invade,
and as morning approaches the harmony fades.
For I am the Keeper of the "Be."
I am the symphony, and I am free.

Fate is heavy-handed on my soul.
Her faceless virtues I must extol.
I know the bitter hypocrisy that surrounds.
Still I rejoice in the wonder that confounds.
For I am the Keeper of the "Be."
I realize that simplicity is the key.

Destiny crowned me. I had no choice.
Now civilization pursues me to crush my voice.
So I speak bitterly, spitting wild thunder.
My mission is to build and not to plunder.
For I am the Keeper of the "Be."
I am heavy-hearted—I am uncertainty.

Try to find me on the plains,
and all you'll see is the lions' manes.
If you look especially close,
I am the bulging vein in the bulls' throat.
For I am Keeper of the "Be."
Both fear and rage abound inside of me.

Little Ditty

Open hand, fly away,
gone forever, another day.

Heavy head and dry mouth,
Sandman says to head south.

And the truth slip slides away,
light breaks and shocks the day.

Mighty (Words to a Song)

Mighty I
Mighty She
Mighty He
Mighty We

Though mortal, Mighty I
Though frightened, Mighty She
Though lost, Mighty He
Though crazy, Mighty We

The mighty seraphs watch us, an awesome panoply.
Still the mighty feelings, unique, wound them invisibly.
For they cannot comprehend the dimensions in our lives –
a tear, a smile, a gasp, far mightier than knives.

You? They?
Mighty, too.
But ask me not how (don't be high brow)
They must figure it out
Jump, wiggle, and fuckin' shout
Jump, wiggle, and fuckin' shout

Mood Swings

High moods, but slow steps,
longing for the time when I know what's next.
Filled with joy and then comes rage,
can't see the stars until I'm on stage.

Just when I think I've calmed myself down,
my blood boils and my feet move the ground.
My life is difficult 'cause I make it that way,
still I can't stand the fuckers that live for today.

Shock surges when I analyze my feelings.
If I acted on instinct I would bring down the buildings.
Yet with control I suppress my primal urges,
but what of those who can't, all Earth's human scourges?

I am no different…I tell myself so;
only that way can I make my little mind grow.
Solemn, stern, stolid, all bone,
if I don't learn to love, I'll die all alone.

My Lady

My Lady writes to tell me about her day.
Such joyous news, and I feel so far away.
Her words reach through the screen and grab my heart.
"Where are you?" she writes.
She needs someone to scream at and to hug.
I smile, and then in a melancholic mood the cyberworld depart.
"If," the rotten word, inundates my mind.
Stop, think how, and the answer you will find.
I call, but she is out sharing her glee.
Oh god, if she only knew the colors she paints in my mind.
When I see her I will tell her. That scent! I can almost smell her.
But perhaps first I shall grab her, reach out and really nab her.
For words cannot convey, my thoughts they would betray.
Oh I must let her know that the feelings she cultivates in my heart be not my own…
Her beauty.

Simply Rose

She thanks me sincerely for the rose,
But am I the reason from the ground it grows?
Water goes to water, and life goes to life,
happiness springs from freedom, and laziness breeds strife.

Apathy is the seed of our country's new wealth.
like the honeysuckle in the spring,
it grows with incredible stealth.
And with no bloom it eventually becomes sterile, green
  indifference.

In the garden the seraphs guard god's roses.
Quadroons are pricked by the thorns of beauty.
In the dark three words come so easy.
Light will raze the dim ignorance.

No, thank you for the rose...I will simply be.

1997

Never in the Moment

I tried to steal you for inspiration, while standing at the station, in the valley of my home.

And though it was not bad—in fact the best I've ever had—I now know the terror of my error.

If you could only see how I shudder when my thoughts recoil in search of my muse—god I'm confused.

I wonder if I'm a traitor, so I ask the addict if I've hit my nadir—*No Answer.*

Now as I lay alone to sleep, but not yet that deep, I search for consolation.

Should I see her again, maybe now but maybe then, I would ask to share her inspiration, while standing at the station, in the valley of my home.

Brilliance

How fragile is the true me?
The tide licks the sands, people on the strand, raging is the band.
All round me is wealth; keen are those who have it.
Practice stealth and you may have it, but beware those who grab it.
No, never mind me, how fragile is the true me?
Work sucks me in, keepin' busy in the raging din.
No need for money, except maybe to find a honey.
That lust kills the feeling, awake staring at the ceiling, say your prayers kneeling.
Wealth would kill me. How fragile is the true me?
Notice the difference in the people: skin, hair, eyes, steeple.
It takes so little to sway me, don't forget the late fee, ass-out and crazy.
Wanderlust a nemesis, how fragile is the true me?
Precarious as falling in love, tighter than a leather glove, simple, white, floating drug
Change for its own sake or not at all, variations in the design are the artist's call.
To find happiness in chaos is no small task, eternity in the present and the person behind the mask.
I'm told that there is a right way, each day.
The gods favor those who die young.
How fragile is the true me?

Her name was Sally Ride.

Her name was Sally Ride.
Deep thoughts she did confide.
In a song, a verse, a word;
so powerful her voice, though seldom heard.

Then came the day when she rolled the dice,
went to LA where it's always nice.
Met some people and played her tunes;
they offered her the sun, the stars, the moon.

She agreed to put her soul out on a disc,
a successful venture, though an awesome risk.
As certain as a wanted kiss,
her brilliant talent could never miss.

Though I have not seen her since the move,
her deep lyrics still cut my groove.
And I wonder if I ever had the chance,
would she even grant me just one dance?

Now I hear people say that Sally sold the farm,
met the devil and borrowed his charm.
But most people aren't quite so pensive,
Sally and I are both real sensitive.

Instant Refund Toast

To Instant Refund's past success,
and to a future even brighter.
To Carroll, Stan, Charles, Chris,
and to Floyd who's quite a fighter.
To cold and snowy days,
and nights that are even longer.
And of course to all the problems,
and to Tom Glaze, who makes us stronger.
To Daddy (Fez) & Mommy (Robin),
and to all the Instant Refund staff.
May IRTS make a million,
and kick some H & R Block Ass!

RED land

In the morning just before day breaks,
fading shadows enter softly and dance till he's awake
His mind's so clear he admires their serenity,
but what of his lost muse off to join the enemy?

Life is seamless; life is sore
Images of last night seep into every pore.

Her silent path wilts in the blazing sun
Gone forever the sweet taste of her tongue.
She has no beginning and does not end
Where can she go? Where has she been?

Life is seamless; life is sore
Images of last night seep into every pore.
Pen in mouth and fire in mind,
he dreams of a land absent in time.

His anger grows but his courage wanes,
wounded at heart, on him life gains.
She has no beginning and does not end.
His love won't bring her back home again.

Life is seamless; life is sore
Images of last night seep into every pore.
Pen in mouth and fire in mind,
he dreams of a land absent in time.

Silver Sliver

I'm in a:
Screaming, silver sliver.
In my mouth a taste so bitter;
Through my bones I feel a shiver.
Heavy thoughts must be considered.

All around me are:
Sleepy, silent sailors
in a creepy, crowded cabin
trapped thick among the willows,
and the puffy, floating pillows.

I can see:
Sweet, serendipitous sleep.
If you can fly no need for feet.
Lost for them like a golden chance,
eternity only a weapon of religious trance

Can't you hear the:
Sardonic, simple song
with no possibility of right or wrong?
Why can't I enjoy their bliss?
Beneath me the engines hiss…

South Dakota Song (The Lingering Pangs)

My lust for her is as strong as ever.
My love not so great, my ties I sever.
Physical boundaries I long to explore.
Could there be harm if she approves the deal?
Moot thoughts besiege me. How I long to feel.
Consciousness rides me…I am so sore.

1998

A Departure

The tanned leather hide
hangs from my wrist,
a woven gift unwillingly, unwittingly
given by a bovine creature.
All the same, the suffering foregone,
the thin, sinewy straps have taken
new life among the hairs of my arms.
Beads woven into the design
add spice to this new life,
and the bamboo shoots, over
time, warped by water, and fall off.
What does it symbolize?
Anything?
Would I trade it for a Rolex?
Probably not—that would be something to worry about
I don't worry about this.
Like me it simply is.
So I'll proudly wear it,
let the world change and tear it.

At Dawn

On a street corner in any old town
the clickity-clack and the city sounds,
Stands my fate and she's all alone.
The blood in my veins just turns to stone
As the rusted wheels in my mind whirl and buzz.
They tell me about love and all that it does.
I try not to hear all of their crap
for my salvation lies in that lovely sap

Though the cold rain begins to pour,
I leave the dryness of my sheltered door.
Soon her name will leap from my lips.
As the music plays my hands fall to her hips.
Then in the morning the dawn of our love,
she and I will be like hand and glove.

Craziness

Moping, Melancholy, Madness
Strong, Silent, Sadness
Hungry, Hollow, Happiness
Yearning, Yawning, Youthfulness
Talking, Trying, Treasonous
Wanton
Wild
Wonderin'
Whisperin'
I see the notes.
They don't spell "music."
I can only hear it if you sing it.
"Are you a seraph?" asks the angel.

Depression (1)

Being smart is of little consolation,
and so increases my isolation.
Then with the rain comes gray depression,
a smiling face, but furtive aggression.

Dickens

I must thank Pip for that simple thought.
I do not think it ever occurred to me.
In a world so crazy and shallow with rot,
letting someone love you sets you free.

Grandpa

There's a peaceful love in letting go
my soul a brand new day.
A mortal man I love so much
has up and flown away.

I can pitch four or five hundred miles an hour.

I can pitch four or five hundred miles an hour.
Don't be sour.
I imagine you could do the same.
What do you mean insane?
It really is quite simple.
Let go the limits.
See the world through a lizard's eyes.
Surprise!
Go without those shackles.
Lay them aside.
That thought only serves to make you human.
Over the horizon the sun is loomin'.
That old crap is a tool for the unwise,
so powerful it keeps the masses in line.
But don't be fooled,
for it is they their chains entangle.
Forgiveness of base imperfection leads to personal
  insurrection—Wink!
Just walk away.
Ahead the new day.
A swing…
and a miss!

Journey

A luckier man I know not one,
afloat in a marsh, on his hip a gun.
Daddy haunts me, the eerie echo in his head.
With heavy heart his journey he doth dread.

He longs for the sky a California Blue,
and in his lover's eyes the very same hue.
The sun will burn the swamp mist from his mind.
Gone are the shackles that so long did bind.

Kerouac (1)

I read on because I am not sure if it is complete and utter brilliance, or the ramblings of an intoxicated, depressed, and spoiled neo-intellectual.

Perforce.

I want to believe it is the former.

We are not so different.

A haunting suspicion makes me suspect the latter.

How arrogant can someone be to think their stories of young over-sexed, irresponsible, junkie Americans hold the keys to salvation of humankind?

Let alone make a living at this?

That I understand...Capitalism makes little sense.

Still the plight and onus of the artist does not escape me.

It is I.

Allowances, no, open-mindedness, brings acceptance and soon appreciation.

How come there is no mention of our attempts to purchase and hoard natural beauty?

Natural, Physical, Temporal

I turn the page.

Kerouac (2)

No Kerouac tonight, or dinner for that matter.
A little ice cream from the DQ and some iced tea will have to do.
In my head are so many possibilities,
I'm frightened by it all.
Like holding water…don't squeeze…
A sacrifice here…there…
When…Where?
The top is my goal.
I'm filled with such soul.
Here my feet on the ground,
treasonous thoughts do confound.
Grasping, rasping…don't want to let go (spill!) all the
opportunities.
But I must rest.
Way past midnight,
skip Kerouac's insight.

Limitless

Happiness is the dreams that fall into space.
Three hundred years past is endless naturescape.
Grueling is life when opportunity is missed,
Guernica your soul when your lover is pissed.
Chaos is the future of our uncertain path,
idyllic the gods and their self-serving wrath.
Hope is a medallion laid into my soul.
Greed is the bacteria that creates a hole.
Nowhere is the course upon which I write.
Limitless is the goal, therein my delight.

Lonely (1)

Lonely, alone, wealthy and unfulfilled,
life in that shell has got to be hell.
My hand against the wall and the other holding my brain,
out through my eyes I let my soul drain.
I've got no direction…I ain't got nothing to lose.
Might even trade my paycheck for some extra time to snooze.
'Cause whether I'm working or sleeping, the dreams are the same.
Can't wait for the day when I've mastered the game.

Lonely (2)

All is good in our techno-prosperity.
I don't want to be alone when I am despairing.
With greater men I shall even the score,
take mine standing, a gentleman the more.

Lonely (3)

It's over…
no longer a slave to my misgivings.
From what hell these doubts arose they are returned.
Almost a crazy man, a lover spurned.
What's to worry? I have but one life to give.
The river is rising—I choose to live.
Silver Socket Sets
Shiny Saddle Shoes
Soft, Sultry Skin

Melancholy

The digital song dances in my head.
Material wealth it offers to spread.
Down this path do I want to be led?
Analytical chains are what I dread.

Meta (1)

Oh how I long,
when I hear that song,
to become one with it!
That's just a thought in my crazy mind,
here on Earth serving a lifetime.
Wanna hear another?
Sometimes I wish I were the only human on the planet,
and for a moment in space that's the case.
Pop!
Again one of six billion…but individual.
There are so many stars.
Bizarre.
I can name a lot of them…no matter.
Peace I find in my soul.
That is my goal.

Meta (2)

I have a vision:
A world of precision.
There is no decision;
no need for revision.
My soul in collision.
I've made no provision.
Enough.

Metabolic Craziness

No, not a maze, a smoggy haze.
Roads looped, paths layered, gates open.
Which way to go?
I am so slow.
Your breath is heavy—a lack of oxygen?
Don't ask such questions, rather offer suggestions.
I don't mind the work, but I hate to suffer
metabolic craziness.

Money (1)

The coin falls to the table.
Click…click…click…heads.
It reads "In God We Trust."
So goes our legacy.
There is no legitimacy
without money.
Don't our laws seem a little funny?
Everywhere I go,
everything I see,
becomes a dollar sign to me.
Let's write a little song
and take it to the bank.

Many of my friends speak Money,
but I am not affluent;
although I could make that my goal.
When I was younger
everything I did had the purest motivation.
Ovation!
Now nothing I do with my day
is taken seriously without thought of pay.
I walk the tight rope of sanity.
The Gold Standard holds only calamity.
Can I have both
material wealth and infinite scope?

Morning

A pop and a click,
then the spinning of a disc.
Out come the words,
the sounds of the birds.
Are you given to fly, or have you got a wish?
I rise with the melody and then I fill my dish.
Tea, lemon, sugar and out the door.
I leave the man for the business whore,
making my move in the morning rush.
Turn up the radio and I can't hear 'em cuss.

Philosopher

What do you think a philosopher is?
Images of old fellows flood the mind.
The Greeks surely follow.
The depressed…God is dead.
I am and I write.
Words give my thoughts flight.
I see the dove and I dream of love.
I cross the river and know its lesson.
It is for me that our earth beckons.

Primal Love Feeling

My yearning is so intense,
my awe immense.
When I see you my pulse races,
the lust it chases,
A primal feeling now grows unchecked.

Silly Sally

Silly Sally Sipper
with the red and yellow zipper.
Oh how I want to trip her!
With my boot I sure could flip her,
but I think I'd rather kiss her.

Snake Bite Eyes

Snake bite eyes in a blue wave trap
breeze in my hair as the sun burns black.
Many different styles strewn for miles,
balls in the air, chartreuse flare.
Toes sifting the stuff of transistors' glass,
feeling lost in the world. Will this too pass?

Song of Plastic

Song of plastic, stream of thought.
The movie reminds me of our predatory nature.
Can we conceive of a life that is not violence,
a being benign to all other life?
The train out my window is squealing to a stop,
Olean, cars, coal—currency of the regional economy.
And so ends El Dia del Padre.
I have closed the book on Mardou.
Conscious thoughts recorded, I dream of polyethylene.

Sputtering Genius

Brilliance breaks across my bow,
a crashing and cracking wave in glass.
Wide I steer of smaller minds,
a captain at twenty-five…
My course altered,
my path adjusted,
only in the physical…
By the idyllic…
Consumed by the tragedy of their lives…
Too eager to embrace their death…

Tax Season

Chaotic brother
I know none other.
When the whistle blows,
when the bell sounds,
when the call comes.

Where's the glory?
Heard the money story?
I want the recognition.
Can't spell it with numbers.
Ah, my talent slumbers.

Wake! Wake like spring born from winter!
My mind will splinter!
The contract honored,
I will explode upon my path,
leaving pebbles for the revenue agents.

Trains

Click. Clack.
The train on the track
The groaning cars.
The morning stars
Smell that diesel
The horn cuts the air
Rust falls like rain
And the wheels come to life
Now the semaphore is green
The gate falls in line
All's runnin' along just fine
The train on the track
Click. Clack.

Who's to Blame?

Who's to blame? What a shame!
Such excess makes me nauseous.
You look out. Try looking in.

1999

!

If she wants me to stop she must ask,
but I don't think she will.
Love…perhaps.
Passion the culprit,
insatiable my desire. I breath fire.

@Houston

Who are you?
Who am I?
I look up.
You compliment my eyes. ("You have the most beautiful eyes!")
Very nice.
Your kindness burns straight through to my core.
Without even another word, I could promise my eternal love to you.
(It wasn't just the words; it was your face. You smiled when I looked up at you.)

A.S.

Do you really want to be remembered,
dragged through the ages and dismembered?
Arrogant men scar the Earth for immortality.
Still she forgives this pretentious formality.

Now suppose that I die without even one dime,
rebuked by eternity, scorned by all time?
Such a freedom is rare, even to the last.
So sweet is the dream, I am left near aghast.

But I bet if you'd let me, I could give you a kiss,
make you forget all this nonsense in sincere eternal bliss.

Charma

Why can't I find a Dharma,
the type who will disarm ya?
Perhaps it is my Karma,
or my stranger brand of charma!

Fraudulent Deity

She makes me feel like a deity,
albeit fraudulent.
She seeds my mind with metaphysical germs.
They grow wild on fertile ground.
She reaps, nay steals, the harvest from my heart,
and I am empty.
Seduced,
I love her stinging wonder.
She fears my illimitable spirit
and refuses, refuses, to acknowledge my human desires and frailties.
I guess she will not make love to gods…

I am

I am
too tired to share the brilliance.
I am not
afraid to fall in love.
I know
this guy in California who is.
I know
this girl in Ohio who is.
(I must
complete a thought!)
I doubt
they have much else in common.
I told them
love is one million emotions,
guided by Fate, policed by Devotion,
I hear
fear, uncertainty, and despair.
I am angry!
Check their list of excuses:
she sings without reason;
good will he abuses
!

My Day

I've got lots of spiders in my room.
Before I even think about it my thoughts go zoom,
and I am running in the woods.
Through my head fly "shoulds" and "coulds,"
and coasting in to my surprise,
a four year old holding my first prize.
I take the daisy and thank her kindly.
Then proudly I walk to my car, but also blindly.
I strain to pay attention to all the folks,
while in my mind I laugh at my buddy's jokes.
Next I'm in the car and out on the road.
In front of me a beautiful woman I behold,
For now the highlights of my day are told.
I see her in the mirror to her left and to her right,
three images to compose her fairness.

Scared Stiff

This fear of dying can never last.
Like you on Earth it will surely pass.
And all that's left is dust and bone.
Perhaps a name, too, carved on a stone.

Sonnet Blue

Bright and blue, so chilly too,
came to your door and evermore,
Stunned was I by your beauty through,
Emphatic praise I delight to pour.

A key to turn, then rubber burn.
Out on the sea, just you and me.
A laugh, a smile, the story turns,
then quietly I sip my tea.

An hour early, but nowhere to go.
Not sure of God but inspired by Fate,
we delight a common thread to sew.
How much longer can I wait?

The songs are magic and the timing right,
I think we could dance all damn night.

Water Tower Love

Are you always so pretty?
A smile…A blush…Oh my!—A tear.
Here come seven smiles in seven styles.
There are no superlatives in life
except you.
Ours is a love affair.

2000

Beep

Beep…
Beep…
Beep-Beep…
Beep-Beep-Beep-Beep…
Do you think you're better off alone?
How do you ignore this urge?
Someone please talk to me…
No hay palabras. (There are no words.)
Beep…
Beep…
Beep-Beep…
Beep-Beep-Beep-Beep…
Oooooooh…

Document3

The wind blows fiercely tonight
and I can't get close enough to you.
Who would have thought that happiness lives in the desert?
Who wouldn't mistake this place in my heart for Babylon?

I turn my thoughts over and over.
With dry lips they say, "Come and get it."
Touching you is electric goose bumps in sweet honey;
your smile, white-golden pearls in crimson candy.

I dive into your waters without a care.
Tears, clear and salty, are washed away.
I can feel the mountains below us.
The flowers on your tongue invite the bees.

Calm meadow grass lies still in the silver moonlight;
you whisper, "Let go your heart."
The frantic city surges in our consciousness,
the feeling punctuated by the lonely cry of the coyote.

Like hushed cymbals we are calmed.
Lying on a soft bed of ferns among the ancient timber
your butterfly eyes powder my nose with musty aromas.
Do you always purr at the end of a dream?

Rejected Titles

Freddie Killed the Cat
As Long as it's Free
A Little Something Different
Semi-Automatic
Rogers & B:Drive
Soup for the Sideburns
Ophelium, Ophelia
B:Drive, B:Drives—masc. 2nd Decl.
Meatloaf Tuesdays
Write by Night
A Tribute to Aaron Feuerstein of Malden Mills
It's Not My Gift to Dance
Shave Me
B:Drive and the Seven Dwarfs
Green Tobacco
In B-Minor
And So It Goes
Beyond the Crystallized Collective
As You Might (See Things)
Killer
Sacrilegious Red Grapes
Rewind
Gotcha! (Got You)
Full Ahead (Forward)
Singing Into a Bell
How I Work
Epiphenomenon
Brain Chemistry
Conceptual Imprisonment
Mechanisms
Quite Simply
Nickel
Based on a Linear Model

Looking For the Blue Oxen
All Perception
Thick
How It Works
On My Back
Method
All Together
Prelude
Pomegranate
Savage Innocence
What Would Witter Do?
Writing Uphill
Poor Man's Radio
On The Verge of Ice
A Technician with Feeling

BULL HEART

A personal and poetic journey through the process of divorce...

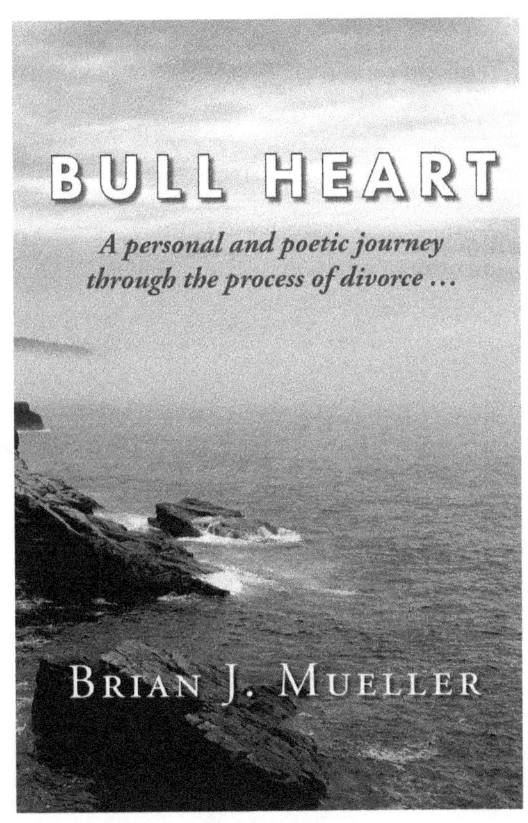

I don't think I was a whole person until my heart was destroyed.
—Marc Maron, host *WTF Podcast*

*To God who loves everyone and everything without fail,
and for all those who strive to do the same (albeit imperfectly).*

Contents

Bull Heart Introduction

Thank you for picking up this book. I take great pleasure in sharing my thoughts and feelings through writing and other creative endeavors. In the case of these poems I am humbled by the sadness and the spirit that set them loose. It was not my intention to write a book of poetry as I mourned the end of my marriage. This is simply how my emotions poured out. Regardless, I hope in my words you'll find a human resonance that affirms life and our connectedness, even through the pain and the suffering.

It may be hard to believe the end of a marriage that has been failing for some time can come as a surprise to anyone. Yet when my wife made her decision, I was still busily working on myself and on our marriage. Then she left me with no choice in the matter, and I had to let go.

Like a concussion grenade, the impact of divorce left me stunned and disoriented. I was overcome with grief, living away from my home, and burdened by responsibilities. After a couple of weeks the reality and permanence of my personal tragedy came into focus. At that moment I was completely devastated.

In the beginning there was little I could do but get through the day. I was faced with very practical decisions and tasks. I did the best I could on all fronts and peaceably said goodbye to my wife and the life I had known for several years. I then limped through the holiday season, after which I moved back to my hometown. It was then that the deeper healing began.

Accepting the end of my marriage was a profound step for me towards letting my life fall apart. For several years I had been questioning my path while working honestly and earnestly toward change. Little did I know the change I anticipated would be so overwhelming.

There was precious little to salvage from my marriage. I was drained physically and emotionally. It seemed the best possible outcome was for the old me to die, and so I stood in the road and let the grief overtake me.

These selected poems chronicle my journey through grief and despair to the point at which I am again standing on my own two feet. Today I am humbled, though in some ways stronger and more deeply connected with my life. I have not arrived anywhere nor am I on my own. Throughout this period of time I have reached out and accepted the support of a great many people who have taken their own voyage through pain and tragedy.

There are so many sources of profound experience and wisdom in the world it is impossible to list everyone and everything upon which I have come to rely heavily in my continued efforts towards growth and renewal. Nonetheless, I hope I can add to this bounty and inspire others as they struggle through divorce or any of the tremendous challenges life presents.

Brian (2014)

SECTION 1

"Midway through life's journey, I awoke to find myself in a dark wood."

—Dante Alighieri, *The Divine Comedy*, Opening Stanza

Lake Pontchartrain

I come to your shores,
my back to the city,
to ground myself.

I, who am drawn to the desert
stand here scanning your waters.

In the distance the clouds gather,
your waves swell.
I watch the storm
pass right through you.

My Testament

I did the best I could.
I remained present.
I was faithful.
I did the work of describing my feelings.
I altered my expectations.
I kept my good intentions of causing no harm.
And most importantly,
I never stopped loving her.

I recognized
how overwhelmed she was,
not privy to my thoughts and intentions
even as I offered them.

I guess it appeared to her as if
I was being destroyed from the inside out,
spirit devouring the flesh.
For me it was a torturous baptism into awakening,
an excruciating initiation into staggering transformation.

The demons that practice madness
are mostly gone now,
I remain, more or less the same in form,
entirely different in spirit.

Loss redeemed me.
When I turn back in anger
I see a marriage smoldering in ruin.
The smoke made more pungent
by her infidelity and greed.

I turn away and back again in forgiveness.
I see a good and honest man
altered by life and by God's love.

It will never be right.
This deeper understanding brings me
into union with all life.
Now heading in the direction of the light,
I am given the grace to let go.

Christmas

My wife decided more than a year ago
she didn't want to be married.

Too hard.

Yeah.

So was divorce.

Last year I wandered around
like a shell-shocked soldier
clutching my heart in my hand.

It didn't stop beating
but turned a deeper shade of red.

This year I'm putting it in a box.
gonna wrap it
and re-gift it to myself.

Gift Life

I knew my life was good,
but I wanted to know I earned it,
so I went to school to learn it,
took a job to work it,
found some books to read it,
gave it away to receive it,
married in order to love it,
lost it.

Until…

I fell
naked
into it.

Like a Bull

I stand alone in the shade;
the world I observe is chaotic.
Like a bull I wait patiently,
suppressing all of my urges.

Some can see it; others cannot.
Breathe in, breathe out.
The breeze picks up.
I feel a surge.
My pulse quickens, I isolate a beautiful woman in all that noise.
Her pants are so tight they reveal the contours of her lower half.
My yearning makes me grimace.
Life, not this woman, is beckoning me.

The stillness of this spot is so seductive
I want to remain here forever.
There is no pain from confrontation.
There is no pleasure from connection.
I must reach toward a greater love,
and risk falling into serenity.

Transformation

True healing is transformation.
It is a gift primarily given by self.

Can it be earned?
It is a grace arising from life's journey.

Can it be refused?
It will call again undaunted.

How will I know I am transformed?
You will feel it. Others will see it.

Are we talking about death?
Merely acceptance of it.

So I must be willing to die?
Again and again.

SECTION 2

"Sometimes, in a summer morning, having taken my accustomed bath, I sat in my sunny doorway from sunrise till noon, rapt in a revery, amidst the pines and hickories and sumachs, in undisturbed solitude and stillness, while the birds sing around or flitted noiseless through the house, until by the sun falling in at my west window, or the noise of some traveller's wagon on the distant highway, I was reminded of the lapse of time. I grew in those seasons like corn in the night, and they were far better than any work of the hands would have been."

—Henry David Thoreau, *Walden*, Chapter 4: Sounds

My Divorce Story
(The Journey)

I stand alone amidst the corpses of my memories and dreams.
There will be no reconciliation of what happened here.
I steel myself for a journey.
My heart again beating;
where is my mind?

Grief

Sadness lurks in the dark hours of early morning
until I push it away.

Every day begins this way,
a little more, a little less.
As the sun rises I start to forget;
then in the pile of mail I see your name,
and like Sisyphus I labor to find peace.

El Divorciado

Am I breathing?
A shallow breath
stumbling in darkness.
Flash! A blinding light.

Days drip by,
indistinguishable.
My heart burns.
Why am I cold?

Alone in this desert,
dry, only dust,
not even a mirage;
am I a ghost?

A soul gone missing,
shells on a beach,
merry-go-round,
littered side-street.

Surrender your badge.
Bleed no more.
A bee stings,
a snowflake melts.

Soft wet lips,
steady, rhythm drum
¡Vaya con dios!
Life marches on.

I'm Not Impossible

I don't know what I thought would happen.
I'm tired of being tired and unsatisfied.
Nothing will ever satisfy me;
I know this because she told me.

There's a place in each of us, deeper than any ocean,
where the undertow is so powerful
we are all moved beneath the surface.

My heart is full.
I love and am loved,
this I never forget.

Still I'm searching for the kind of fullness
a man my age knows
comes only from within.

I got the message clearly:
If life was easy everyone would live in bliss.
Still, how much is grace and how much action?

Thought

I shape my world with thought.

If I had never uttered
the word divorce
in the presence of my ex-wife
she would not be thus.

It makes me wonder just a little bit about
the vindictive human spirit.

Coldest Mornings

The coldest mornings are the clearest,
the light brightest on the horizon.
A friend tells me this crisp weather makes her feel alive.
Me too, if only to keep warm.

My pain arrives at the appointed hour
on these chilly mornings.
Only one other person possibly shares it,
but I don't know her any longer.

These feelings are too heavy for me alone.
So I sit on this bitter cold morning and add them to my poem,
or I go to a meeting and insert them into my conversation.
As I grow in strength and wisdom, divine alchemy makes them
love.

Say a Prayer for Me

Words are oft times my greatest comfort.
So please say a prayer for me,
that I may loose my grip on this diving bell
and float back to the surface
like thousands of tiny bubbles,
that I may breathe the air no matter how cold and dry,
living among others,
accosted by vandals, pick-pocketed
as we move from one glorious place to another.

Fire

I carry an ember,
hold it out,
coax the flame with my breath.

In the light I see many faces
similar to my own,
each carrying a stick
they wish to ignite.

Where once I stood guard
now I stand back.
Make your own fires.
Just know this is not the truth.
It is a mere spark
of the eternal flame.

Falling Apart

Am I difficult to live with?

This heart is full of love,
my intentions true.
So what drove me crazy?
Could it have been my loneliness?
A marriage with too little for me,
requiring every ounce of my being,
an inevitable collapse?

Darkness is an unholy beast,
sustained and nourished
by feeding upon itself.

She would collapse into bed in the early morning;
I had been awake for hours.

These guys bought us dinner and drinks.
My silence surprises me.

January

I wake up to the cold
with a cold.

My life is a gift,
even if frozen
in liminal space.

The warmth of my heart,
always in tune with spring,
holds me.

Hurt

I keep my hurt contained and packaged neatly.
It's greasy and it stains.
And it stinks to high heaven,
reeking of ammonia.

I name my hurt.
I call it bloody, hot, overwhelming, hideous, debilitating, angry,
desperate.
Then I put it back in its box,
tell everyone I'm above it,
that it's not important.

This is my recipe for forgiveness,
because a part of me thinks I must.
And I tell myself it takes a big heart to survive.

On my shelf is a shiny box heavy
within the proverbial polished turd.

Now is the time
to root around in it,
show it to myself and to another,
allow it to wash over me like a waterfall
until the box is empty.

Forgiveness

Holding the pain is like running
with a handful of water,
wetness evaporating on the pavement, or joining the soil.

Feet in the mud I stand strong against the breeze,
add compassion to my list of names,
call my tormenters to task with gratitude,
exalted by the blood gushing out of my heart.

First a vacuous silence,
then a chorus of shrieking Harpies,
next a rock speaks to me, and then a bird calls my name.
A hand reaches out for me, another and then another.
I grab fingers, hands, wrists, forearms, shoulders, torsos.
We embrace.
I am human.
I am alive.
I am forgiven.

Adrift

I am not alone in knowing
What it feels like to be yoked
to a partner unwilling and unable
to fully give herself to another.

Generous people share their stories with me,
their own journeys through uncertainty.

A wisdom and grace more powerful than my will
cast me far from shore;
alone I drift.

The unknown surrounds my little raft.
I fear being overwhelmed by the unpredictable current.
Then the wind whispers in my ear, "Surrender to me."
With no course to plot, I say a prayer for life.

Annie

I gave you all I had.

I accept your decision.
Our marriage was failing.
I failed.

The pain is humiliating.

Scars form and then recede into familiarity.

I say a prayer for your deepest well-being
and I wish you happiness, safety, and peace,
so that I may reflect on my own with gratitude.

SECTION 3

"In all of nature, no storm can last forever."

—Lao Tzu, *Tao Te Ching*

Field Theory

Energy
surrounds me
then confounds me.

Closest as I wake
in that lucid state;
my dreams bring past into present
untangling my reality.

This energy of being,
more elusive through effort,
fills me with light,
creates the words on this page
as I dissolve into awe.

Release

Letting go is my grace.
It comes without toil, a breath,
an exhale.

I wake when it's still dark.
A fire truck rolls by.
Engine brakes roar, the red water dragon stops.
Then it growls off who knows where.

My breath returns.
Along with some sadness.
An opera scene opens in my mind
filled with large boulders.
A young tenor sings tales of woe
While the wind chorus,
carries them into the air.

His words will never find their intended,
and even so would be unintelligible.
Still he sings
until his breath gives out.

An exhale:
forgiveness returns.

Toward Pain

Move toward the pain,
smile if you can,
laugh even.
Just do it;
you won't be sorry.
God Almighty it hurts!
White hot
dull
then sharp
suffocating
almost completely
overwhelming finally
stillness.
Is it still there?
Of course,
I can still feel it,
though a little less.
Still familiar,
I make friends with it;
we have an understanding
called serenity.

The Journey Is Me

Tears form,
and my heart turns to lead.
My departure date is approaching.
Why go?
Why indeed.
Why the rain?
Better yet, why Wall Street?

Am I not content?

There is only one true answer.
"Yes, and…"

No two trips are ever the same.
I go with an open heart, an open mind.
Though I go out into the world,
you know it,
the journey is me.

A Humble Light

I carry a light with me like a flare.
It's mine,
a spark of truth—
not the whole thing.
Some can see it, though I haven't shown it,
and I can see theirs.
We nod, maybe even share the warmth.
So it goes…

We nurture or neglect this tiny light
as we choose.
It grows brighter
joined with others.
I'll never forget seeing her light the first time:
unfamiliar and fragile.
Who knows what she thought of my light?
She mistook it for the truth.
I guess I wanted to believe it too,
I agreed to the lie,
smile,
wink.

Soon enough came the rain.
First slow,
then steady,
inevitably a deluge.

My flame went out.
Seeing this, she took her flame,
departed.
Mine wasn't the truth after all.

How do you live without a light?
How frightening it is,
to feel the darkness coiling around you!

Finally
I consented to die
then begged for a pardon,
said a prayer for humility.
And almost as suddenly came the light of others,
along with the love to relight my own.

Overmatched

How I ever got fixated on you,
I can't say for certain.
I write the words
and I know this is bullshit.
You were just the right mixture of pretty and sweet:
the perfect cocktail.
I drank, and drank, and drank.

I got sick.
What can I say?
I wanted more.
You didn't have anything else behind the bar.
I got lousy.
I just wanted some water,
a moment of peace,
anything.
Instead you took it all away…
first the sweet drinks,
and then you to pour them.

Cold turkey wasn't my choice.

Neediness

You didn't need me
but I needed more of you.
Life seemed easier for you
when you found me.
For this, I was happy.
A gift to be able to give.

So little remained to nourish me.
I turned to a higher power.
"Humility," came the response.
My proud heart balked.
You watched confused,
certain I was going to die,
'cause I told you that's how I felt.

You increased your distance,
finally stealing away.

If this is a gift,
I thank you.

Gratitude

Shifting my focus
back to me
ends the violence
of imposing my will
on others.

It defines control narrowly,
accepts love unconditionally,
removes judgment
as it returns me to calm.

The rhythmic thumping of my heart
marching toward exhale:
this is the ecstasy,
that the prophets wrote about.
(My beautifully imperfect life,
how is it not intended to be so?)

I belong!
We all belong!
There is only pain
when we deny our humanity,
the bond of love with all of life.

How can I feel anything but gratitude!

Never-Ending Journey

So much whooshin' through my head.
Like the two beautiful women,
both of 'em my age
at the party last night.
Both of 'em with somebody else.
The one folksy from rural Indiana:
she's got deep eyes and a tattoo.
Something tells me she's flirted with death.
I like her boyfriend.

The other has heard of me,
knows my nickname,
seems to like me already,
her husband legendary, blue collar,
salt of the earth, not meant for a suit.
She looks to me like a politician's wife.

I feel an empty yearning,
I want, I need, I feel
in no particular order.

I thought my salvation was a woman.
Drunk Rick asks me soberly,
"Is this your first time going through this?"
He's had more than his share.
I'm embarrassed to admit it.

Drunk Rick knows what I know.
The pain is the only real thing.
My ex has buried me.
Reality doesn't get any more stark
unless you add blood.

I'm hitting the road to let go
(some more).
It's a warm 29F.
Your life is this journey.

Springfield

Springfield, Missouri
or thereabouts,
dawn is still a couple hours off.
I wake in my rental car,
my first night at a KOA.

It was chilly,
still not too cold.
A sleeping bag and my cap
worked well to keep me warm
on a crystal January night.

In the distance red lights flash
delineate the smokestacks of a power plant.
Every hour a train horn shatters the silence
as a two-hundred-ton diesel thunders past.
Neither can drown out the stars.

I am lonely, not alone.
This part of my journey,
at times eerily quiet,
is abundant with life, with love,
as I travel with my higher power.

Mea Culpa

I hope she has forgiven me,
says an occasional prayer for my well-being.
I need this from everyone I've wronged,
no one more than myself.

What do you do when you've done the unforgiveable?
You forgive yourself.

I still sometimes wonder.
Why must I be forgiven?
The answer does not come so easily.

There is stillness after any great tragedy
a fire, a tornado, a divorce.
I had to lose what I thought most precious
to comprehend the value of my tiny life.

I held tightly to my honorable manhood,
the mythic marriage of my making.
Not even death could've saved me.
My salvation, my redemption, my forgiveness:
my insignificance.

The Rawness of a Broken Heart

To touch,
be touched,
to hold,
and to be held.

Just being in this world
increases my yearning.

I got the relationships I deserved:
a marriage based upon neediness,
six years that emptied my soul,
then abandoned me at my darkest hour.

The rawness of a broken heart
keeps you alive
just so it can be felt.
It keeps others away,
forcing you
to really reckon with it.

Go to war with a broken heart at your own peril.
Just let it defeat you.
When the fires subside,
when you exhale your last breath of resistance,
a calm ensues.
In this moment your heart
may again accept the seeds of love.

Belonging

The world is enormous.
It took me less than a day on the road
to be reminded.
I glide over hills and into valleys
the highway an endless, unbroken path
of dashed lines and painted signs.
I belittle the distances
even as I catapult further into the abyss.

Three days are gone.
The road is the same.
The trucks are the same.
The diesel rumble is the same.
The stores and businesses are the same.
The food is the same.
The questions are the same.
I am the same.

The people are a little different,
otherwise, they're just like me.
They are me.
They drive like me.
Walk like me.
Eat like me.
Rely on their phones like me.
Stop at rest areas like me.

I said hello to a smoker.
He admitted driving was hard for him,
just like me.

Eating at Indian Casinos,
camping at KOA,

talkin' to whoever will talk,
livin' life closer to the present,
I see that I belong,
somewhere, anywhere, right here.

The Importance of Sleep

By day
I keep my fear
my cravings
at bay.

Fatigue,
nightfall,
and the constant tug of loneliness
prey upon my peace of mind.

Preparing for bed
it is all I can do
to keep my demons
contained.

I close my eyes
my heart trembles
as I invite the pain.
Move closer
so I can see you.

I inhale deeply
hoping to take in
the love that is God.
If I sleep
I will see my fears anew.

My Attention

My life is less
about any one thing
than it once was.

This realization comes, like so many,
in a moment of respite
alone and moving deliberately.

My mind always active and powerful.
What is noise, what is ego?
Is my awareness a curse?

I recognize big things as they are happening.
I notice seismic shifts
though it takes me time to articulate them.

How authentic is my awareness?
I once doubted it
not understanding how it connected me to my life.

I tried to turn it off and couldn't.
I sought distraction to subvert it.
I made it stronger.

Alone, a little cold and uncomfortable,
I relax into my humility with a deep breath,
at ease with my transformation.

Precious Stillness

Sitting in the dark
reading about death and resurrection.

I'm given pause
as I think
to my own biological imperatives,
to the women I've known desperate for a baby.
Is this really life yearning for life?
Or is it a general desire to truly be alive,
human beings in a modern world,
desperate for authenticity,
searching in all the wrong places.

My gift
to have traveled far
has brought me only inches closer to the truth.
My learning, formal and informal
are all hints, cosmic guideposts
pointing to the present moment,
the precious stillness.

Alone in the dark,
the rattling of the heater,
outside it's 18 degrees.
Inside I am warm.
I surrender to my life.

Passages

What time is it?
I ask frequently,
almost immediately
as I emerge from sleep.

I am truly sorry
if I have wielded time
like a bludgeon.

The more experience I accumulate
the past comes into perspective.
And with this articulation
I fill with dread.

What happened to my youth?
Such questions seem trivial,
quaint reminders of eighteenth century enlightenment,
or that guy you sat next to at a bar.

But this is big shit,
fucking, death and infinity.
It all fits equally well
into a pint glass, or the Grand Canyon.
Redemption a bit of gravel in your shoe.

The sun and shadows
are my favorite representations of time,
the displacement of light and dark
on all manner of shapes and surfaces.
This is my life.

In this one last moment
before the next,
I add my humble reverence
to the appreciation life has for itself.

At Night

The mythic me falls apart.
The brave warrior,
the stolid intellectual,
the peaceful philosopher,
the clever wit,
the lone gun:
they all go.

When the loneliness comes,
the wide open desert darkness,
terrifies me.
With its wind and space,
the forest darkness
envelops me
with its dense branches and strange sounds.

I lock myself away,
biding my time
until morning.
I will survive.
I will survive.
I will survive,
to see the true me resurrected.

Inevitable Death

The war can be ended unilaterally.
Just call the whole thing off.
Immediately the struggle will be over,
life and death brought back together,
a soul in union with the Universe.

It feels strange
at odd hours of the night or day
to contemplate my recent death
knowing its inevitability,
the necessary step
in my own resurrection,
the revelation of my naked humanity.

Oh, how I fought it!
Along the way resenting those
from whom grace flows so easily.

I thought my love was special,
ambrosia of the gods,
my unique gift to bestow
in the tiny world where I held dominion,

Fortunately it was I
my poison killed,
and the true me
it returned to this world.

Newlyweds

I see the familiar rings
on the anointed fingers,
and the more familiar patterns
of togetherness,
newness.

A window into my past,
a glimpse into your future.
Mostly it's just uncertainty,
and a little jealousy,
finally a wish
for your happiness
as it comes through growth
and an abiding love.

SECTION 4

"You will either step forward into growth or backward into safety."

—Abraham Maslow

The Love You Bring

Just as there is no virtue in suffering,
there is none in proving
the limits of someone else's love.

As suffering creates growth,
so too does the realization,
grounded in our humanity,
that love is infinite.

From time immemorial,
all living creatures,
and indeed all of life,
have known God as love.

So go bravely.
For wherever you perceive a void,
it will be filled
with the love you bring.

Abundance

Why is it so hard for me
to fully comprehend,
to internalize,
the abundance of life?

Why indeed.
I have seen it.
I have been gifted it.
I have even offered it.

I must remember this,
when pain and sorrow come calling,
displacing feelings of peace,
taking with them my sense of abundance.

Seeds of Sameness

Out on the road
there was a clarity,
a more rational being
in the moment,
my path a little straighter,
the view more distant,
existing not by thought,
alive.

In this state I came
more fully into myself.
Nudging me forward,
with my imperfect voice,
to sew the seeds of sameness.
With whomever,
with whatever,
whenever.

And when I began to long for home
I was reminded
I am home.

River

There is a great deal of wisdom
a great deal of grace
flowing through the fractured rock of the canyon.

The advancing water carves the stone
reveals ever deeper layers
carries away sediment
all the while spilling out
the loves,
the losses,
and even the ordinary
of my life.

Kelly

Though love is never lost
it comes and it goes
in many ways.

Quick as a chair
pulled out from under me.
Slow as a swimming pool
after Labor Day.

It goes
sight unseen and without a sound
finally crashing in
on a cold December morning.

The Ones to Keep

How do you know the ones to keep,
and the ones who will keep you?

The answer precedes the question:
one part faith,
two parts love.
It is that simple.
So long as you always keep room for pain.

Emotional Sobriety

My heart and mind attach this morning
to my mother's existential sadness
and my desire to eliminate it.

There are countless ways to frame my wish,
most of them burnishing a son's motives.
Still I am awake and clear.
I have grown sober through my own sorrow,
which has made me realize
I have no business meddling with feelings.

My mother's pain preceded me;
it may have even led her down the path
in which I came to be.

Relationship Man

There is a cultural disconnect
written in confused silences
dismissed in avoidance.

The fact that I was unhappy
that through my efforts
to examine the relationship
to understand my behavior
to change myself and to grow
to explore ever deeper levels of emotion,
my marriage ended.

What was confounding
now makes perfect sense,
but that is not my point.
I write this poem for all the men
whose desire for relationship
exceeds societal norms.

There are many women
as broken as any man
numb, hard, cold,
unable to connect to their emotions.

Corazón

My heart just opened
like a dropped egg,
no witnesses, only silence.

I think it kinda funny now
how it kept doin' what it needed to
in order to keep me alive,
spilling out only grief, spreading only compassion.

Backfire

I told you I loved you so often
it lost all meaning.

Three simple words,
one tiny declarative,
passionate as rhythm and a red dress,
solid as a granite boulder,
painful as the longest, most difficult day.

The *I love yous* I sent,
not always the lightest gifts,
wrapped as they were in my needs,
changed me forever as they were returned.

So I opened them for myself.

Another Departure

There is no avoiding my pain
and yet I try.
There is some consolation in knowing this
even more in the way struggling binds me
to my humanity,
to all of life.

Today I leave my home again,
saying goodbye to my parents,
wishing my friends well,
thanking all the familiar people.
I am not
I could not
without them.

Equally difficult
is to remain
fixed.
My hometown grounds me
then pushes me away
a gateway to a larger world.

I pray only
that I follow a calling,
going forth to spread and to find love,
never turning away from those who need me.

No Matter

The details
don't matter to me
anymore.
Old fireworks,
bursts of energy in my mind and body,
explode in strange narratives,
colorful dreams.
They are a fading light,
and then they are gone.
The sulfur smell lingers,
then is blown away.

My lifetime
a blip in the cycle.
How can anything matter more
than my belonging?

Nostalgia

When the days gone by
return in my dreams,
familiar faces, strong emotions,
I awaken heartbroken and a little confused.

The repetitions of these moments
are farewells,
the urging onward,
a great push from the Creator
toward the inevitable fulfillment
of my life in this Universe.

Truth

I don't know is a release,
an honest look in the mirror,
a way to continue creating my life.

Click!

Time is not a camera,
even as moments are frozen in my mind.
Click!
That rock face contains the history of one hundred million years.
Click!
My face contains the story of forty.

Samsāra:
the cycle of life,
or is it the cycle of suffering?
This morning I embrace my suffering,
welcoming thoughts about my mistakes,
mourning the losses.
Why not own them?
As if there was a choice in the matter.
As if the details really meant something.
Time is not the camera;
I am.

Lighten Up

If connection
through life
through consciousness
is the rational order of the Universe,
why do I feel so disconnected?

Standing on the shoulders of ancient mystics,
Yoda said:
You must unlearn what you have learned.

(If this does not enlighten me
to take life and myself
a little less seriously,
nothing will.)

Progress

As I grow older
my body offers more specific instructions.
First in subtle ways:
what not to do,
what not to eat and drink.

And of course I resist
even though I want to feel good,
to be at peace.

Joy has never come
in my resistance to anything,
especially with regard to my physical body.

Though I often resist,
I now hear my body urgently telling me
to eat and drink well,
and as I do these activities,
to listen to for more instructions
in the present moment.

No Turning Back

The road leads me everywhere,
past the trees
into the desert
back to the sea.

The road well-worn but unpaved,
mile after interesting mile,
I get stuck in mud.
Or I must stop to empty gravel from my shoe.
I pass strangers,
some kind,
some carrying even more than I.

The road has no signs, no markers.
There is no sense of urgency,
no shortcut,
but plenty of roadside diversions
buzzing with activity,
tantalizing the senses,
urging me to indulge my hunger.

The road is my constant.
Though I am changed,
when I am lost, struggling to let go,
without judgment, it shows me the way
and the wind whispers, "No turning back."

Unconditional Love

My heart goes out,
and I find it easier
to connect with children,
when they are around.

They are not fixed,
unable to be rigid.
Except in their momentary desires,
they remain open to the world.

To be around them fills me
with peace, with hope, with love.
Even as they demand my attention,
there is nothing I can do to resist.

I watch others relate to children.
They too are drawn in magnetically.
Yet no one can get as close to them as their mother;
they are her innermost expression of love and creativity.

Still that love exists within me,
given abundantly by my own mother.
I feel it deeply, groaning as it pushes me
ever outward toward love, toward connection.

"Yes, and..."

How glorious it is to be alive,
to feel the spirit of life moving
in all its mysterious ways,
the peaks and depths of my existence.

And how joyous it is to write.
The emotions that move my pen,
difficult though they may be,
verbs, nouns, adjectives, create serenity.

Try as I might
there is no way to subtract
only the pain from my being.
Life begins and ends with *and*.

Simple Gifts

There is so much beauty in the world
I find myself turning away,
closing my eyes,
trying to suppress my need
to possess it.

Those blue emotive eyes,
the smile of a child,
the winter sky reflecting a rainbow,
the right tool for the job,
the sweetest bite of cake.

I want to own it all,
and failing this, to simply be a part of it,
to know my own beauty,
perhaps share it in verse,
a gift offered in humility.

Surrender

I read the words aloud.
Two others listened,
how I came to understand God,
love, the creative genius,
my broken path to reunification,
to fall apart,
completely
(or not at all).
Resurrected with uncertainty,
yet unable to go back,
my life will never be the same
(thank God).

Empty

No words remain
to describe my marriage,
to parse the lessons hard earned,
to give my broken self one more lament,
yet another moment to be wronged.

I'm empty.
Those difficult feelings have moved.
They find other pain to validate
before yielding to the present moment
and on down the road.

If I ever turn back in sadness,
it is because the present demands the attention
I am unwilling to give it
while resisting the light of creation,
until I breathe in the love that surrounds me.

Love Immortal

There is no end to love or else
the God within me should die.

I have tried to become indifferent
and cannot.
Even when pain tempts me toward hate,
it is ultimately love,
in a kaleidoscopic panoply,
through which I exhale.

Wanting to Get Better

Which is to say wanting to grow,
to change,
in a new direction
advertising new destinations.

I won't get there with a wish.
A new course
requires new behaviors.

The pain of growth is real,
yet no more real
than the routine behavior
of stubborn resistance.

The way forward is paved,
well-traveled,
already within me.

Groundless

A life put on and worn
can be brutal.
Even if by all appearances it seems serene,
indoors, a tempest.

The *I* that is my ego
never wanted to let go,
never wanted to let things fall apart,
only knew the concept of self preservation,
could only measure loss.

That *I* is dead.
Remnants remain in my pain,
then float away like clouds.
I wake in groundlessness.

I feel lighter than I have
since I was a child.
And though the innocence is long gone,
tears create the mud
which covers me in forgiveness.

Even as I am born again
my senses as strong as ever,
remind me where my pain resides.
So I go deeper to the love that is my being
and connect to that in others.

First Light

At first light
it seems
today is about sadness,
the sudden waking
to an upset stomach,
grumbling,
arousing old pain,
picking at wounds.
But it needn't be so,
everything turning over,
melting even,
like snow becoming water,
and dripping away.

Love is not lost.
And so this day begins
with a blink,
with an exhale,
with a hug,
even with a headache.

Silent People

There are some feelings
akin to my pain
I cannot touch.

It frightens me to think they are too near,
though that isn't quite right.
It seems they are fading
into forgiveness as I let them go,
or that I never really knew them at all.

I have a tremendous capacity to feel.
Life gives me empathy and intuition
through which I often find myself
face to face with God.
And still I cannot see into the darkness.

There are feelings attached to people
I wish to bring closer.
Their silence is a fortress.

I step back.
Just naming pain
is like taking a drink from a fire hose.
We must drown a thousand times
before we learn to live under water.

Balloon

My grieving has come to an end.
Words about my marriage are difficult to write.
Where despair once moved my pen,
the reservoir of pain is running dry.

From time to time dark clouds surround me,
but they bring no more than a drop or two of rain.
I embrace my pain, understand its yearnings,
as it returns me to the source of our connectedness.

I fell in love and held it
more tightly than a child to a balloon,
expecting it to carry me to new heights,
tripped, let go,
it flew away without me.

What a balloon it was!
Divinely given,
but only for a moment,
so that I might open more deeply.

Dante Deo

Something stirred the pot this week,
a fact I hate to admit,
a conversation with a friend,
or maybe the bourbon last night.
All I know is I've stumbled backward.

Again today I woke suddenly,
a little too early.
In my dream a woman I loved
carved off a piece of her own ear,
yet it was my ear that bled, I who felt the pain.

My image of God creates me,
my love takes form in this world.

Who knew how painful it would be
to put down my shield,
how exposing those vulnerable parts within
would bring humiliation, transformation, resurrection.

The daily grind to move forward
through very little joy, mostly discomfort and pain,
an honest regimen.

When I yawn awake each morning
a groan I make
as I continue to be created.

MORE BULL

Songs of serenity and surrender...

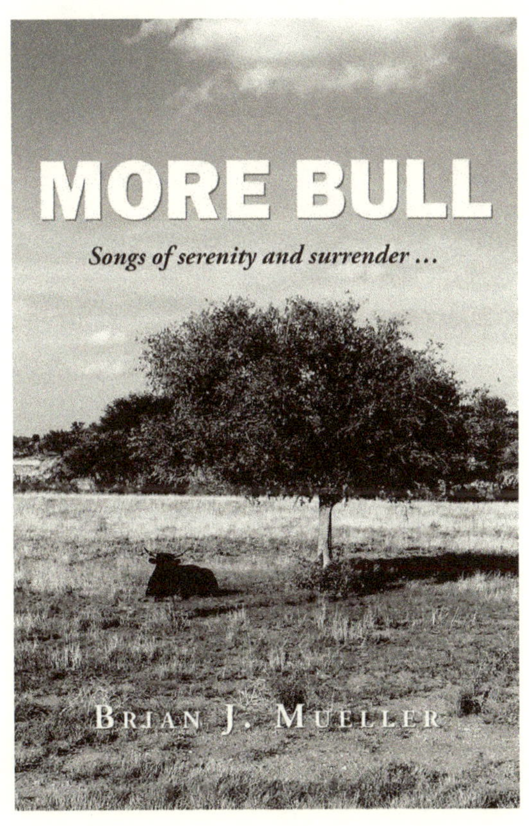

"We do not think ourselves into new ways of living.
We live ourselves into new ways of thinking."

—Fr. Richard Rohr, OFM,
Center for Action and Contemplation

To my good friend Joe who gave me the title for this collection,
and ever reminds me to laugh and enjoy my life.

Contents

More Bull Introduction

Thank you very much for picking up this book. Reading and writing poetry has become part of my daily ritual. I get up early each morning and make a cup of tea before finding a place to sit quietly. I try to enter the new day slowly by reading, sitting and contemplating. Some days it is easier than others. Eventually I put my pen to paper and draw forth words from my feelings and the inspiration of others. These are some of those words.

One way to get better at something is to do it. This is part of the motivation behind publishing my third collection of poetry, *More Bull*. My previous collections *Bull Head* (2002) and *Bull Heart* (2015) opened me body and soul to the power of poetry. I quickly learned through writing I have more access to my thoughts and feelings. As I continue to write, doors are opening to new perspectives and to an entirely new way of seeing this world I could not have imagined even just a few years ago.

The poems in *More Bull* are selections from *Brian's Poem of the Day*, a project I began in July 2016, through which I share a poem each day of the week with subscribers to my email list. (Learn more about *Brian's Poem of the Day* at http://poem.digitalalphabet.com.)

Some of the poems contained in this volume go back as far as the 1990s which were very formative years for me as a new college graduate learning to make his way in the world. However, the vast majority of this collection was written more recently as I traveled around the country and undertook a personal transformation which continues to this day. From my new state of mind and heart came a flood of poems dealing with being human, examining life, learning how to live, relationships and dying.

Wherever you are on your journey in life, I sincerely hope my poems resonate with you. I don't believe they would have so much meaning for me if they did not reflect the teachings and wisdom of so many others. I have learned a great deal by opening my heart, and in doing so I've been drawn closer to others and to a greater understanding and appreciation for all of life.

Brian (2016)

BEING HUMAN

"My first world is humanity. My second world is humanism. And, I live in the third world being merely a human."

—Santosh Kalwar, writer

Sensors

God help the born sensors—
those who feel every tingling,
so much so their hair betrays their thoughts,
and their skin predicts the weather.

I know sensors.
I am one of them.
There is no escaping the sensory overload.

This world is both satin and sand paper,
sonic booms and silent symphonies,
blinding light and opaque night,
incense and garbage heaps.

Longevity is terrifying to the sensor who wonders:
Will my senses fail?
Or will I feel every arthritic joint,
as my world falls dark and silent?

Redemption is enjoying these sensations,
knowing that our perceptions of them
are nothing more than passing glimpses of God.

The Voice

Sometimes I grow tired of my own voice,
not the one you hear,
the one deep inside.

That voice is sometimes hard and unforgiving,
urging me forever this way or that,
relentlessly seeking for me the perfect life:
free from want,
free from pain.

Me and that voice,
we never get there,
to that imaginary clearing
where the grass is always green,
the breeze gentle,
and the sun forever shining.

We just grind along
the way we always have.
Though more and more I pause
and just feeling my own breath,
I know that voice is not me.

Too Hot

Hot, humid smothering weather…
Why is that cricket chirping?
We all go from air conditioning to oven.
What could this be doing to our insides?

I turn away and think of the dark forest,
a dense thicket of greenery
concealing a spring fed pool
rocks covered in green moss
air as cool as the first night of autumn.

I love the sun and summer.
As a boy I knew the heat and humidity intimately.
We slept all night in each other's embrace.
Now we have only contempt for one another.

Words

If words were food,
I could cook something magnificent.
If words were flowers,
I could fill this room with scented color.
If words were feathers,
I could make a giant, comfy down pillow.

Words are wounding.
They make thoughts real.
Words are healing.
They offer forgiveness.

Long is the history of
the words which fall out of my mouth,
of the words which spill from my pen.
I believe I know my words well,
yet I do not control them,
or understand fully their power.

If there are a thousand doorways to the Kingdom of God,
words surely are the key to one of them.
How humbling it is for me to admit,
I do not possess this key even though
I have held it.

The Flow

I love all things which flow,
their flowing a gentle reminder
of when I have blocked my flow,
of when I would rather hold my life
than be living.

We create these pools at our own peril,
making our lives muddy and stagnant,
withholding the flow from those downstream
as if we can ever fully control the grace which is life.

I am among the broken branches which clog our waterways,
the parts of me broken and spindly
catching on leaves and on others
making quite a mess.

First time and then prayer have smoothed me
from the inside out.
Now like a piece of driftwood
I am cast about in the flow,
or sent to the shore to watch life float by
knowing even in the ebbs
I am never separate from the flow.

All Shall Be Well

I would like to commission a symphony,
having it tell the rather ordinary story of my life,
and of my death,
through an array of musicians
coaxing their instruments to an exultant crescendo,
before crashing into the still vacuum of space.

And when no sound remains,
except for the expectant cough
or the creek of a chair on stage,
the conductor will turn around and say:

All shall be well.
Go forth and love one another!

Yes's and No's

My ex-wife had *joie de vivre*
of which I was quite envious.
She said yes to everything
whether it was good or not.

Her simple acquiescence to life
intrigued and frightened me.
She naively let all kinds of ghouls and goblins in the door –
the same door I entered.

It all worked for a little while,
her persistent yes's,
my pragmatic no's,
until it didn't.

Then on the night she said no,
I said yes!

Beechwood Ave.

In 1985 the spirits in this house were different.
They held me in their bosom,
while supporting a young family
full of energy, innocence, and vitality.

Like people the spirits come and go.
Today this house feels somewhat empty,
though the memories linger on…
If only the walls could speak.

There is a certain sadness in witnessing change.
I am unable to resist it,
becoming forever a part of it,
bearing both its weight and its light.

I pray to move as the seasons do:
  slowly and assuredly.
I know change inevitably will find me,
yet I beg for mercy on my wounded soul
and for patience in doing God's will.

More than forty years we've traveled together;
the old and the new spirits
always coming and going.
They lead me in an unbroken circle,
with Love as our light and our way.

New Day

Feeling hungry, thirsty, tired, then awake,
watching the sun move across the sky,
hearing the songs of the birds carried on the breeze,
while the sweet smell of decaying leaves brings me home.

What a gift it is to be alive!
I say:
What a gift it is to be alive!
I dance but do not even know it.
Every cell in my body vibrates to the hum of the universe
as it sends out the loving message we call creativity
in a mystical Morse code.

I want to sing and to praise life.
I want to thank God for my precious, tiny life.
I want to let go of my hurt and pain,
letting the river carry them away.

This is my song,
written for a new day.

No Hearts to Break

I will not waste another moment
crying over those I have lost
lest my pain become too precious
and your pity the oxygen I breathe.
It is enough for me to say I loved them,
and to be believed.

Brothers and sisters,
humans and animals,
animals and nature,
what of our memory will exist after eons?

Forever is the heartbreaking beauty of this earth,
of this universe,
as it settles into eternity
where there are no hearts to break.

Step Four

Am I willing to look honestly at myself?

Is there any other way,
once your heart has been broken,
once you have fallen,
once you have come to a dead end?

A good look in the mirror requires humility,
a healthy sense of humor,
and then the strength of steel
to look inward,
really peer into those dark spaces,
taking inventory of what you find there.

Fear, fury, failure, frustration,
all parts of the experience,
until that moment arrives,
the searching now complete,
with no unexplored places left to map,
you see your world anew.

Journey of the Radical

If at some point in your life,
(as is true for me on this very morning)
you do not wake up alone,
whether quite literally without those relationships you've come to expect,
or rather so deeply connected, you are singularly overwhelmed.
Then it stands to reason you have not fully awoken.

My generation now comes to middle age
as all must
on bended knee,
wounded,
befuddled,
perhaps amused,
the men not crying,
the women not even crying,
scratching their heads.
thinking: *we were promised jetpacks*;
sighing: *but we knew it was all bullshit.*

My own fallen soul is so battered and cynical
it confines me to hell,
a solitary existence full of bad dreams,
memories returning with gifts of bitter resentment.

No matter what your what is,
none of us are condemned to a living death.

With love I acknowledge and let go of my wounds
day by day,
brick by brick,
so carefully, so laboriously deconstructing
the walls I have built around my being,

keeping from my soul the essential grace
which sets life free in its quest to join God.

Staring at the rocks in the desert
I glimpse eternity.
My own struggle,
our struggle is so important.
And yet it makes me chuckle.

Now, imagine standing on a beach
wave after wave unfolding.
That is you, me, our generation, our species, life:
endless waves.

Life ascends only insofar as it is necessary for us to fall.
It is easy to rejoice in the flesh.
We do this so effortlessly for which I am thankful.
But now is the time to join soul and flesh.
This is the journey of the radical.

Good Enough

I am inspired by petting a dog
or drinking a glass of strong iced tea.
I think this is what it means to be alive:
to rejoice in the simple things,
like a good, strong hug,
like an afternoon walk,
like that laugh you share with someone
when you recognize those things you have in common.

There is ample complexity in life
which I mistook for a riddle to be solved.
But thank God for the humiliating experience
which led me to the edge of my resourcefulness.

You can take all I know about the Universe,
and it wouldn't add a grain of sand to the Grand Canyon.
Still I know I am somehow part of it all.
That's good enough for me.

Trading Hardware for Software

I fell in love with a computer—
Windows95.
Do you remember that?
Mick Jagger singing, "If you start me up,"
as the mouse pointer *clicks*
the new START button.

I fell in love with a computer
and maybe that's all good,
for it was innocent enough.
But what I really wanted
was to fall in love with a woman.

My computer knew the sad story,
how she wasn't that into me,
how I loved in vain,
how it was all megahertz and megabytes for me…
at least for the next few years.

Eventually the computer lost its luster.
Over many months and many miles
I gradually grew up.
I traded time in front of the screen,
for walks and movies and holding hands.

Though I fell in love with a computer,
it just wasn't meant to be.
Now we just work together.

Humility (and Grace)

Humility is a steaming pile of shit
on a bitter cold morning.
It's the day after day of waking
to a life of pain and confusion.
It's the leaky faucet, the missed phone call, the dead end job.
It's the screaming baby, the tone-deaf in-laws,
and the realization there's nowhere to turn.

Then comes the moment you fall down
right where you are,
bury your face in your hands,
squeeze out a few tears,
pausing for however long it takes.

Stumbling…
Crumbling…
Bumbling…
Crawling around on your knees,
humility the only means of standing up,
towards letting go of whatever you're holding,
not acting as if nothing has happened.

Real transformation requires humility,
the ability to reach out to others in our nakedness,
to ask them for help,
so that we may take our seat at the table,
in communion with love,
with life,
with God.

Acceptance

I'm a bit apprehensive this morning.
I want to write a brilliant poem,
still my words don't always come out just right.
So I invite acceptance to sit down with me.

Acceptance is a gracious guest,
always welcome,
with a standing invitation.
Like me, I hope you'll come to realize,
acceptance is what makes choice possible.

I accept this may not be the best poem I've written.
My simple surrender allows the words to flow.
Here on the page is my heart—
my love for all of you.

What I Want to Be

I am a poet—
fanciful artist
somber fashion plate
decorator of emotions
false prophet
good friend
forlorn lover
preventer of forest fires.

I speak with an accent.
I write with a culture bias.
I have a penis.
But I don't forget a woman gave birth to me.

What I want to be
is genuine—
to love and to cherish my life,
to author life in others,
and as I fall asleep,
to be held in her arms
assured God loves me.

LOOKING AT LIFE

"In our life there is a single color, as on an artist's palette, which provides the meaning of life and art. It is the color of love."

—Marc Chagall, artist

Back to Work

Back to work! barks no one.
Yet we return to our desks,
doing whatever it is we do,
the nudging-pushings-leanings,
all the little actions that move this economy.

Nobody I know says do it.
We just do it.
No matter what the weather,
we try harder.
When we ought to make love and eat bananas—
we work.
Then we drink,
fill our tanks for $1.99 a gallon,
and repeat.

The next big thing will be when we ask ourselves why,
bring this relentless locomotive to a stop,
and vent the air brakes in one collective sigh.

Fall is Coming

Steel yourself.
Take a jacket for the road.
Fall is coming.
The sun will seem to grow dim.
The days will become shorter.
The air will smell sweeter with the scent of decaying leaves,
and the breeze will bite a little harder.

Now picture yourself riding in a balloon,
any kind of colorful balloon,
rising against a blue sky,
fluffy clouds drifting by,
as you let go a deep sigh of contentment
bidding thanks to the beautiful scenery.

Some say it is the seasons which give life its meaning.
Some say it is written in the stars what you do,
what you'll become.
I think it is a great mystery,
my every breath and step
a profession of my faith.

Jazz

Jazz,
with its strange beats
and broken rhythms
practiced alike by
mathematicians and
the high priests and priestesses
of smoke-filled,
and gin-soaked back rooms—
the urban night forever summer and sultry.

Jazz,
the language of dreams
the random firing of synapses
deep inside my head
the cacophony of a world gone mad
the syncopation of love between twinkling stars
horns exploding in my subconscious
while the rat-ta-tat-tat of the high hat
lulls me back to sleep.

Jazz,
how God speaks to me
without words
without any order known to humans
like the predictable unpredictability of love
the wind from God's trombone
blows in all directions
all improvisation and swing notes
calling us to common purpose.

No Country for Old Men

This is indeed no country for old men,
nor a place for young men in flip-flops.

There is not enough beer, liquor, wine,
to smooth these jagged rocks,
to tame these angry snakes,
to seduce a gentle rain.

Men and women alike
become quite small here
through seeing great distances
and watching the play of light
slither across the ragged landscape.

It all means precious little
if we do not take the sun
and shine its light inward.

Too many years in the desert
leaves spots on our faces,
the wind blowing dust and pushing up wrinkles
until we take our place among the fallen rocks.

A Matter of Perspective

This month of August,
it seems a little bit longer,
maybe hotter, too,
or at least more humid than July.

Lately the sun willingly surrenders the sky
to angry clouds and torrential rains,
while the ground drinks happily of all the water.
You can hear the corn growing taller,
and the mowing crews cussing and hustling.

There's always something happening,
no matter what time of year.
The temperament of people consistently changes,
just as the Earth is forever turning and tilting.

More often now I'm noticing other humans,
and animals, and all the living things.
I've stopped worrying about remembering the day.
I don't want to anticipate the seasons or
count the years.
Keeping track of life is a dubious privilege.
Real luxury is a cool day in August,
blue skies—an imaginarium full of clouds.

From where I sit summer seems to be fading.
Yet somewhere else, maybe in Australia,
in a town I cannot pronounce
there is a man my age.
We are rough reflections of each other,
and for him spring is just beginning…

Silence

When there is nothing to say
do not invent words,
do not fill the space,
let your tongue rest,
then listen in the stillness.

You may hear little but the breeze
or you may notice the surrounding bustle.

No matter what,
the din will never fill the space.
The universe is so vast
no utterance of humankind
can transcend time or space—
only the silence.

A Good Poem

A good poem wants to be sticky.
Not that you'd memorize it,
but for a word or phrase
that goes deep,
a metaphor
that rings true,
an image
you cannot see.

A good poem has room for all the gods,
not just yours—
a panoply of flawed deities
forever bumbling along with you—
chattering
as you sit at the bar,
making you laugh
as you kneel in church,
waiting patiently
as you sleep through your alarm.

A good poem does nothing
the sunrise or sunset cannot do better.
It only tells the story
you might otherwise forget,
when you're too busy
to remember her birthday,
when you're too tired
to make the bed,
when you're too angry
to tell him you love him.

Collapsing

I like the word *collapsing.*
It conjures for me the image of something
falling and folding in upon itself.
It denotes the passage of time
and a certain inevitability.

A wave *collapses*
then withdraws into the sea.
The market *collapses*
leaving the investor penniless.
When a lung *collapses*
the victim becomes breathless.

Yet my life *collapses,*
and I am reborn.

Birthday Wish

The pounds and the gray hairs
begin to gather like so many memories.
It's your birthday
and that's okay.
You know the incredible gift
which is your life.
All the stuff you gathered up
has become a funny story.

Be glad for the sun.
Be glad for those clouds.
Be glad for the moon and the stars.
They are glad for you.

Love is Growing

Somewhere in the shadows
and on the cold wet ground,
love is growing.

Yes, love is growing!
Look around.
Look under.
Look more deeply.
Open your heart and you will see,
there is nothing in this world but love.

Love is in the rusty tin can by the road,
and in the nearby muddy tread mark.
It is in the dead tree lying along the path,
alive and crawling around with the worms.

Love is forever looking at you in the mirror.
How did you ever fail to see it?

Field Theory

Energy
surrounds me
then confounds me.

Closest as I wake
in that lucid state;
my dreams bring past into present
untangling my reality.

This energy of being,
more elusive through effort,
fills me with light,
creates the words on this page
as I dissolve into awe.

*First published in *Bull Heart* (2015).

When I Sweep

When I sweep
I try to bring all the crumbs
and all the random things the floor collects
into a pile or two,
or even three.
I then brush these piles into a dustpan
before I deposit them into the trash.

So it goes with my life.
I collect everything,
the ordered and the random,
into neat and distinct piles.
At some point I move them,
discard them,
give them to Goodwill,
or they simply disappear.

LEARNING TO LIVE

"Mistakes are a part of being human. Appreciate your mistakes for what they are: precious life lessons that can only be learned the hard way. Unless it's a fatal mistake, which, at least, others can learn from."

—Al Franken, comedian and U.S. Senator

Intentionality

The purpose and emotion with which you do things is
intentionality.
In my understanding of this
experience has been my best teacher.

I am a man of good intentions
as I am motivated by positive thoughts and emotions.
I know many women and men
with similar good intent.

Of course there are those with bad intentions,
spurred on by negative feelings and beguiling thoughts.
Some no doubt know it;
others are oblivious to their good and to their bad.

I want to see my own heart as true.
I feel the pure goodness of my intentions.
Yet I recognize my own mysterious shadow side,
aligned to its own moral compass and intentionality.

Every day I hope to live more fully
in the light of deed and intentionality,
to spread the joy, love and kindness I feel within,
a tiny flame that burns even in the darkest night.

Let it go whispers the wind...

It is hard to imagine the absence
of that which is present in front of you,
the very thing so obvious and real,
right there before your eyes,
emanating from within or without.

Suddenly it just disappears!
And then,
you too will be gone,
but only that part of you
which would hold onto anything too tightly.

Let it go whispers the wind.
There is plenty of rock for you to stand on.
Just know it too will become dust.

Tell me,
the angel asks,
On the darkest of nights
when there is no moon
and fear grips you in a cold embrace,
what is it that holds you until the light?

Time and my unrelenting experience of it erodes me,
revealing the very soul of the universe.
I am part of this creation—
never ending.

Scoop yourself up.

Scoop yourself up.
The puddle you've become is only temporary
and not very puddle-like—
maybe only in the sense you're reflective,
lying there looking at the sky.

What do you think she sees when she peers into your eyes?
For a single moment everything just stops.
Yeah,
everything just stops.

I said get up and get going!
For what reason did you spend hours
staring at the Cross,
unless to be resurrected for this day?

There is no reconciliation of mystery,
only that something in you which understands
you must take her hand—
take all hands,
and go forth loving this world.

The Love You Bring

Just as there is no virtue in suffering,
there is none in proving
the limits of someone else's love.

As suffering creates growth,
so too does the realization,
grounded in our humanity,
that love is infinite.

From time immemorial,
all living creatures,
and indeed all of life,
have known God as love.

So go bravely.
For wherever you perceive a void,
it will be filled
with the love you bring.

*First published in *Bull Heart* (2015).

Men's Rites of Passage

A man can know too much
filling his analytical mind with data,
which is then dutifully compiled and computed
into the blueprints for a great fortress.

I know this to be true and self-evident,
but not only because I've lived in a castle,
rather the truth found me when I went into the woods
sat naked, tired, and afraid with other men.

Together we listened to the rain falling,
felt the smallness of our being,
finally let go of all that data
which we ground into red meat for the wolves.

There in nature,
never fully wet,
never fully dry,
we wept silent tears
and while listening to the drumbeat of life,
peacefully took our place in the circle.

Pieces

Now that I've gathered a few more pieces,
I wonder if there are so many more,
pieces I've overlooked,
pieces no one has ever told me about.

I once thought life was about order,
everything hinging on the proper punctuation.
Then came a storm,
followed by suffering and a profound darkness.

At last I caught the sound of a beating drum.
It beckoned me to follow.
This is how I learned
to keep scattering those pieces.

The Time

Don't always know the answers.
Shrug like a kindergartner when
someone asks you the time.
Wake up with no agenda.
The only question you ought to ask is:
How can I help?

There is a time for declarations,
but it is not now—
not for you anyway,
and not for me.

Let us loosen the grip we have on our lives,
lift up our souls,
offering them in service and love.

New is the Wind

New is the wind
which has been blowing forever
bringing unseen things
past eyes that do not see,
going through us
as much as it is pushing us
until we go along with it.

Strange as it sometimes seems to me,
there is nothin' in this world needs fixin'.
This includes you,
it includes me,
and everything else seen and unseen.

Furthermore,
if the wind can touch it,
I don't need to worry about it.

Something Else to Wear

You inevitably become
who you think you are,
even in the delusion
of youth,
of excitement,
of romance,
of work.

I became the image of a man
which I was handed
while growing up.

It fit
or it seemed to fit
until it no longer fit.

When the time came
to take off the illusion
(*as it inevitably comes*),
I didn't feel bitter
or even much resentment.
I felt naked and tired,
and waited for awhile for something else to wear.

There are so many options,
yet it turns out the best is to remain naked—
asking questions,
of the sun, the moon, the stars, and the other animals.
Unconcerned as they are with pretense,
you can trust their answers.

Haunted by the Ghost

It's the last day of August.
I'd like to write some cheerful words,
a fond farewell as summer wanes,
a hurrah for the triumphant greenery of Ohio,
along with a prayer for a colorful
and a mosquito-less Fall.

Yes, I want you to know I am well.
Everything is in as right a place as it can be.
And truly,
for whatever else is happening in the world,
it is a fact that all fits this time and place.

Some days are impossibly busy.
Others try my patience to no end.
I wonder often:
What am I doing?
Who am I doing it for?

I am haunted by the Ghost.

This one day towards the end of summer is just beginning.
So why is it I think I should know what comes next?
Everything that really matters holds mystery.
Maybe I'll sit quietly a moment longer.

Leave the Door Open

Leave the door open.
If you have a key
throw it in the ocean.
Don't be stupid and lock yourself away.
Leave the door open.

Leave the door open
and your heart will remain open.
No matter what lies beyond the threshold
your heart can give and receive,
so long as you leave the door open.

Leave the door open
for yourself,
for others,
for love and for forgiveness.
Just leave the door open.

Leave the door open.
Feel the wind swirling in and out.
Let what lies beyond change you.
Be ready to walk through it.
Yes, leave the door open.

Leave the door open
so in time you will become
a great outpouring of God's love.

Don't Go Back to Sleep

You've heard this phrase before:
Don't go back to sleep!

Some days you are frightened.
There's nothing between you
and what feels like death.
So you close your eyes
putting off the inevitable.

That inevitable rearranges the inner landscape.
It pours you another drink to forget,
and forbids you asking questions.

The inevitable can be wicked,
quick to throw a fist or an insult,
even quicker to withhold food from the hungry.

You won't always know what to make of this world.
Everyone who does know has died at least once,
and is then reborn in a million different ways.

Staying awake is onerous.
I can't tell you whether this life is utterly simple
or confoundingly complex.
I lose the thread every time I think I've found it.
Fear will always visit you unannounced.

Remember:
Don't go back to sleep!

God's Pocket

I always put the blue leash on Simon,
the red one on Griffin,
creating order—
or at least creating a color balance,
which means something in my tiny,
tiny universe.

What do you do to create order?
Do you park in the same place?
Eat the same thing for breakfast every day?
Carry your keys only in your right pocket?

Sit down.
Take a deep breath.
You could clean your car or your house today,
but no rearranging will make you feel as content,
as does embracing the chaos.

All of us,
we're just living in God's pocket.

Ever Becoming

Place yourself in child's mind—
see the world and hold it
in the limitless gaze
of one who knows not
the certainty of death.

Yet be not the child
you were once,
but the man or woman
you are meant to become—
ever becoming.

Learn how to love
as God loves everything.
Learn how to be loved,
as God loves you.

PEOPLE

"I've learned that people will forget what you said, people will forget what you did, but people will never forget how you made them feel."

—Maya Angelou, poet

A. Robinson

You crack me up with a clever turn of phrase.
My smile turns up and to the left.
I cough out a laugh
thinking:
I hope to meet you someday.

This awakens the absurd inside of me.
Now I too muse:
How wonderfully strange it would be
to greet others by patting them on their stomachs
or touching their left ear with my right hand.

So I'm guessing your writing has opened doors
and no doubt dropped some panties,
leading to more poems,
and eventually to that hopeless feeling
of spilling ink into the wind.

I think you might be like me.
You come upon the Grand Canyon.
The sheer enormity is preposterous.
So you just sit there laughing,
knowing God is a brilliant comedian,
waiting a little longer to descend
while thinking seriously about a leap of faith,
almost certain you could fly.

Evelyn

There you stand,
alone,
nowhere to go,
overwhelmed.
Thinking, *What is this pain?*
I've never hurt like this before.
Am I going to die?
Am I already dead?

How lucky you are!
How lucky!
And you don't even know it.
Just breathe.
Breathe.
Breathe.

Life has led you into darkness,
to teach you a new way of seeing.
Take that first step.
Go deeper into the unknown.
Follow the path as it unfolds.
Let all the feeling you feel,
pass right through you.

Listen to the words:
I love you.
I love you.
I love you.

You will not be spared your life.
But you are free to offer it for others.

Don

Don often sat for hours,
even for days,
alone in the wilderness.
He preferred to be near water,
but it really didn't matter whether
he sat by a stream
or deep in the forest
so long as he was secluded.

Don died seven years go,
and it's taken me this long
to know why it is he sat in nature.

He never thought to tell me.
I never knew to ask.
It's profoundly true,
some things you've just got to learn on your own.

Sonnet Blue

Bright and blue, so chilly too,
came to your door and evermore,
Stunned was I by your beauty through,
Emphatic praise I delight to pour.

A key to turn, then rubber burn.
Out on the sea, just you and me.
A laugh, a smile, the story turns,
then quietly I sip my tea.

An hour early, but nowhere to go.
Not sure of God but inspired by Fate,
we delight a common thread to sew.
How much longer can I wait?

The songs are magic and the timing right,
I think we could dance all damn night.

*First published in *Bull Head* (2002).

That Old Man Over There

That old man over there—
he used to love the mornings.
You'd see him up early
taking the dogs for a walk,
kissing his wife before work.

Then something happened.
I couldn't tell you what,
but I never saw his wife again.
Winter came and wouldn't leave.
Everything about him turned gray.

Things stayed like that for some time.
Then the house came up for sale.
Goodwill trucks arrived to take the furniture,
and I saw that man pull out one Sunday morning.

That was thirty years ago.
He stayed away quite a while.
There were no kids to anchor him,
no reason for him to be here,
so he went out in search of a reason to be alive.

He must've found something,
or at the very least a way back home.
I've seen him from time to time.
He seems more at peace, very calm.
Now he comes every day and writes in his notebook.

EXISTENTIAL

"I have an existential map. It has 'You are here' written all over it."

—Steven Wright, comedian

Carpe Diem

The clerk at the gas station had *carpe diem* tattooed on her arm.
She was pleasant,
full of energy,
the kind of clerk you hope to have when you're in a hurry.

Now this morning the ephemerality of life comes to mind.
It is an indulgent thought,
the kind I can entertain without regret on a sunny day.
I will be none the worse for noticing the passage of time
or for wishing my gut to be ephemeral.

So it is life moves along.
The sky changes color.
The trees change color.
My hair changes color.
And one day someone or something will be standing on the dust
that was me.

Carpe diem is a youthful slogan.
It doesn't mean as much to me in middle age.
It lacks a certain faith and hopefulness for tomorrow.
What is it we wish to seize?
What would you let go if your immortality was assured?

This House

This is the house.
We accomplished some things here—
nothing more amazing than falling in love.

No nail is insignificant,
nor the colors too green or blue or beige.
Those pictures mean something.
These dogs next to me on the couch too are symbolic.

I want to hold onto this for all eternity.
Yet only God's love is eternal,
as it lies beyond, over, around,
my comprehension.

And forever,
isn't that just another word for love?

Parthenon

There remains a significant part of the Parthenon
piled on the rocks of the Acropolis
in the land called Greece.
Through two millennia the gulls have watched human empires rise
  and fall,
while ever-so-slowly Athena's temple returns to dust.

The Parthenon has no natural enemies,
yet it cannot resist the elements, nor the acid rain.
So the government has taken up preservation,
hoping to prevail against those forces
which would separate the ancient structure
into the very atoms from which it was built.

Surely the architects of the Parthenon thought their structure
  would last an eternity.
Perhaps Athena herself was charged to protect it.
Even so I wonder,
what constitutes forever in the minds of mortal men and women?

Every great builder,
whether she creates with her body, mind or soul,
knows nothing born into this world
can withstand the forces of demolition,
delivered with each heartbeat of a loving God.

A Prayer

A prayer for the weary,
the wounded,
the fearful,
the powerless,
the sick,
and the unaware.

A prayer for the mighty,
the rich,
the educated,
the lucky,
the healthy,
and the vigilant.

A prayer for knowing,
a prayer for surrender,
a prayer for union,
and a prayer for love…

Let us not overthink our lives
lest we provoke our fears,
lest we adopt the fears of others.

Let us learn to behold the beauty of life.
Allow us to be conquered.
Allow us to be confounded.
Allow us to be the very love which surrounds us.

Roads

Today I think of the roads—
all of the goddamn roads I've traveled.
There've been so many roads,
every one leading me to the very place I occupy this morning.

For me the roads are like veins,
they spider all over the place,
yet always lead back to my beating heart.

Along the highways and byways
I've seen things I could never have imagined—
funny signs, quirky buildings, a weather blimp,
bullet cases, broken people, and endless vistas.

The list goes on and on,
as does the road.
Of course not every road is paved.
And there are many ways to follow a road.
Some don't require you to move at all,
only silence.

One more thing…
I tell you this from humble experience:
the road that takes you away
from the being you truly are
is best avoided.

Rapture

When I need to take all the complexity
of this moment,
of my life,
of this world,
and distill it into one simple word,
I speak, "God."

God understands.
God comprehends what I cannot.
God loves where I will not.
God breathes for me when I hold my breath.

I speak, "God, "
until my heart breaks open and the love pours out.
I pray, "God,"
until the courage to face this world moves my body.
I sing, "God, "
until the beautiful song reveals my beauty.

God is the sun's fire.
God is the gale winds.
God is water for the fish.
God is the gravel beneath my feet.

God is all that I am,
all I do not know.

ENDNOTES

Afterword

Hey there Dear Reader!

Thank you for picking up and reading this anthology of my poetry. It is a privilege for me to share my words with you. I truly hope you find my poetry both meaningful and resonant. Please feel free to share this book with others who might also enjoy it. And be sure to share your thoughts and feedback with me through my website: www.DigitalAlphabet.com. While there you can also subscribe to *Brian's Poem of the Day*, delivered each day for free to your inbox!

Acknowledgements

There is so little we can ever accomplish alone. Never is the case truer than in the publication of a book. I love writing, but editing can be an arduous task. So foremost I want to thank my editors. My mother Susan and sister Jenny have always been reliable readers, editors and constructive critics of my work. Undoubtedly, both *Bull Head* (2002) and *More Bull* (2016) benefited from their profound gifts. Also, Kate Kearns of *Black Squirrel Workshop,* was the very thorough and patient editor for *Bull Heart* (2015). I owe these women more than just a word of thanks.

I must also extend gratitude to Adam Robinson of *Good Book Developers* for his keen sense of design and book layout. He made the process of publishing *Bull Heart* (2015), *More Bull* (2016), and now *Complete Bull* (2017) both easy and I daresay fun. Much of the excitement in publishing comes from seeing your printed book. Without Adam's expertise, my collections would not look so great.

To my family and friends, I want to tell you how much I appreciate your love and support. You know what these poems mean to me and to my well-being. I'd also like to thank everyone who reads and subscribes to *Brian's Poem of the Day.* Your notes of support and candid reflections have been an inspiration and a tremendous source of motivation for me to keep writing and publishing.

There are also myriad people I once knew and authors I've at times exalted who've effected my writing. In many cases, I suspect these influences may be obvious. Among the names people will recognize are Ernest Hemingway, Jack Kerouac, Italo Calvino, F. Scott Fitzgerald, Henry Miller, Joseph Heller, Tom Robbins, John Steinbeck, Kurt Vonnegut, E. E. Cummings, Charles Bukowski, Reginald Dwayne Betts, James Kavanaugh, Wendell Berry, Emily Dickinson, Richard Rohr, Bill Wilson, David Whyte, Rumi, Hafiz, and many, many others who may be less well-known or I am forgetting to name…

Thank you one and all!

Also by Brian J. Mueller

Bull Head
(2002)

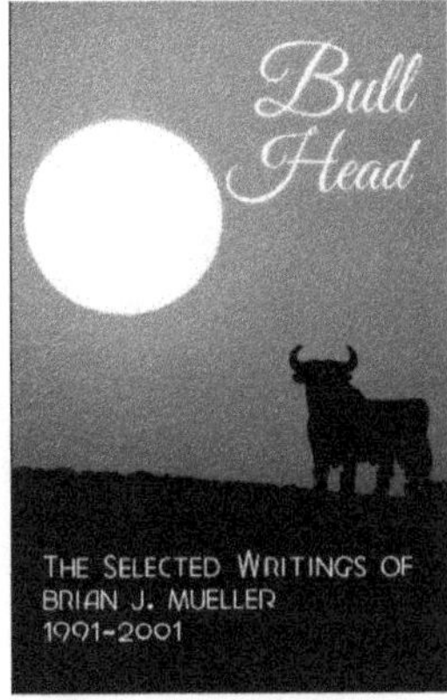

Bull Heart
(2015)

More Bull
(2016)

More information is available at www.DigitalAlphabet.com.

You can find these books at online retailers and order them through your favorite bookstore!

Notes

These pages are for your thoughts and poems…

www.ingramcontent.com/pod-product-compliance
Lightning Source LLC
Chambersburg PA
CBHW032059090426
42743CB00007B/178

* 9 7 8 0 9 9 6 8 1 2 0 6 1 *